The Sublime Biography of the Final Messenger of Allah ﷺ

GLOBAL STRUCTURE OF MAKTABA-TUL-MADINAH

مکتبۃ المدینہ
MAKTABA TUL MADINAH

مکتبۃ المدینہ

MAKTABA TUL MADINAH

Asia

Pakistan
Nepal
South Korea
India
Sri Lanka
Bangladesh

Middle East

Bahrain
UAE
Oman

Africa

Kenya
Uganda
South Africa
Mozambique
Mauritius

Europe

Greece
Spain
Denmark
England
Italy
Norway
Germany
Holland
France

North America

America (USA)
Canada

Australia

Australia
New Zealand

UAN:021-111-25-26-92

P.O.Box: 75300

Aalami Madani Markaz,
Faizan-e-Madinah,
Main University Road,
Babul Madinah Karachi, Pakistan.

0313-1139278

The Sublime Biography of **the Final** Messenger of Allah ﷺ

For the youth

Presented in Urdu by

Majlis Al-Madina-tul-'Ilmiyyah (Dawat-e-Islami)

Translated into English by

TRANSLATION DEPARTMENT (DAWAT-E-ISLAMI)

Te Sublime Biography of the Final Messenger ﷺ

An English translation of 'Aakhiri Nabi Ki Piyari Seerat'

◆

1st Publication: Ẓul-Qa'daĥ, 1443 AH – (June, 2022)

Translated by: Translation Department (Dawat-e-Islami)

Publisher: Maktaba-tul-Madinah

Quantity: 3000

SPONSORSHIP

Please feel free to contact us if you wish to sponsor the printing of a religious book or booklet for the Isal-e-Sawab of your deceased family members.

Maktaba-tul-Madinah

Aalami Madani Markaz, Faizan-e-Madinah Mahallah Saudagran, Purani Sabzi Mandi, Bab-ul-Madinah, Karachi, Pakistan

Email: global@maktabatulmadinah.com | feedback@maktabatulmadinah.com

Phone: +92-21-34921389-93

Web: www.dawateislami.net | www.maktabatulmadinah.com

اَلْحَمْدُ لِلّٰهِ رَبِّ الْعٰلَمِيْنَ وَ الصَّلٰوةُ وَ السَّلَامُ عَلٰى سَيِّدِ الْمُرْسَلِيْنَ

اَمَّا بَعْدُ فَاَعُوْذُ بِاللّٰهِ مِنَ الشَّيْطٰنِ الرَّجِيْمِ ؕ بِسْمِ اللّٰهِ الرَّحْمٰنِ الرَّحِيْمِ ؕ

Du'a for Reading the Book

Read the following Du'a (supplication) before you study a religious book or an Islamic lesson, you will remember whatever you study, اِنْ شَآءَ اللّٰه عَزَّوَجَلَّ:

اَللّٰهُمَّ افْتَحْ عَلَيْنَا حِكْمَتَكَ وَانْشُرْ

عَلَيْنَا رَحْمَتَكَ يَا ذَا الْجَلَالِ وَالْاِكْرَام

Translation

O Allah عَزَّوَجَلَّ! Open the doors of knowledge and wisdom for us, and have mercy on us! O the One Who is the Most Glorious and Honourable!

(Al-Mustatraf, vol. 1, pp. 40)

Note: Recite Salat upon the Prophet صَلَّى اللّٰهُ عَلَيْهِ وَالِهٖ وَسَلَّم once before and after the Du'a.

TABLE OF CONTENTS

Chapter 1

Chapter 2

Chapter 3

Chapter 4

Chapter 5

Chapter 6

Chapter 7

Chapter 8

Chapter 9

Chapter 10

Chapter 11

Chapter 12

Chapter 13

Preface

The final Messenger of Allah صَلَّى اللّٰهُ عَلَيْهِ وَاٰلِهٖ وَسَلَّم is the most perfect and accomplished person in the history of mankind. His blessed life duly personifies the merits of all the aspects of elite humanity. He صَلَّى اللّٰهُ عَلَيْهِ وَاٰلِهٖ وَسَلَّم is not only a Prophet and a Messenger, but also the one who would call towards righteousness, a reformer, an intellectual, a leader, an orator, a head of state, a supporter, an educator, a judge, a teacher, and a spiritual guide; in short, he صَلَّى اللّٰهُ عَلَيْهِ وَاٰلِهٖ وَسَلَّم is a guide from every perspective of life and society. That is the reason why we find complete guidance in relation to every aspect of humanity in his blessed life.

Keeping this importance and need in mind, Maulana Haji Muhammad Imran Attari, the head of the Central Executive Body of Dawat-e-Islami, expressed his desire to the Islamic Research Centre of Dawat-e-Islami for such a brief book be written on the blessed biography of the final Messenger of Allah صَلَّى اللّٰهُ عَلَيْهِ وَاٰلِهٖ وَسَلَّم which comprises of easy-to-understand language so that common people, in particular, children and the youth (school and college students) can read it easily.

He initiated this auspicious project by working on the first few pages of the Blessed *Seerah* and then handed it over to the Islamic Research Centre (of Dawat-e-Islami) for completion.

It is a great coincidence that just a few days prior to Nigran-e-Shura's request, the head of the Islamic Research Centre, Rukn-e-Shura, Maulana Muhammad Shahid Attari al-Madani, established a sub-department under Islamic Research Centre, namely, "The Department of Seerat-e-Mustafa", in order to work on the Prophetic biography as per the need of the time. By the virtue of the benevolence of Rukn-e-Shura, this esteemed work was handed over to this department, who completed this brief book in a short period of time.

Maulana Muhammad Hamid Siraaj al-Madani al-Attari (the responsible Islamic brother of the sub-department "Seerat-e-Mustafa") was privileged to work on this project, whereas, Maulana Muhammad Rashid Ali al-Madani (the vice-editor of monthly magazine, Faizan-e-Madinah) and Maulana Muhammad Jaan al-Madani al-Attari (assistant of the sub-Department "Seerat-e-Mustafa") cooperated fully. The details of the project are as follows:

- First of all, the blessed life of the Beloved Prophet صَلَّى اللّٰهُ عَلَيْهِ وَاٰلِهٖ وَسَلَّم was written in sequence. Subsequently, for the ease of the readers, it was then divided into different parts, compiling it into different chapters.

- Thereafter, the whole matter was referenced, scrutinized (from a *Shar'i* perspective) and compared.

- In order to make the book as easy as possible to understand, an effort was made to use simple words and sentences. After finalizing the book, its content was given to a common person to read. More than 100 words and over two dozen sentences, which he found difficult, were changed into simpler Urdu.

- The initial plan was to present the Prophetic biography within 63 to 92 pages. So, keeping brevity in mind, many events of the Prophetic biography have been mentioned briefly. For detailed biography, please read two books of Maktaba-tul-Madinah, *"Seerat-e-Mustafa"* and *"Seerat-e-Rasool-e-Arabi"*.

- A great effort has been made to present latest information about the places relating to the Prophetic biography (i.e. geographical demographics, distance from Makkah or Madinah, distance by road, climate, current name, etc.). (This information has been obtained from different websites and some Arabic books.)

- All the verses of the Holy Quran have been written in Quranic script and their complete references have also been given. The translation of the Quran by the Imam of Ahl al-Sunnah, Imam Ahmad Raza Khan رَحْمَةُ اللّٰهِ عَلَيْه, namely "Kanz-ul-Iman", published by Maktaba-tul-Madina, has been included.

- Pictures of different places and the maps of some battles have also been included.

- *Shamaa`il* and *Khasaa`il* (the beautiful description and unique qualities of the Prophet صَلَّى اللّٰهُ عَلَيْهِ وَاٰلِهٖ وَسَلَّم) is a golden aspect of the Prophetic biography, and a great model for Muslims. Hence, some *Shamaa`il and Khasaa`il* have also been included in this book. Similarly, at the end of the book, some verses and Hadith regarding the Prophetic glory have also been included along with the information about the items which the Beloved Prophet صَلَّى اللّٰهُ عَلَيْهِ وَاٰلِهٖ وَسَلَّم would use.

- The complete life of the Beloved Prophet صَلَّى اللّٰهُ عَلَيْهِ وَاٰلِهٖ وَسَلَّم has been briefly included at the end of the book under the title, "The Prophetic Life at a Glance".

- In order to avoid any *Shar'i* mistake in the book, *Shar'i* scrutiny has also been carried out by the honourable Mufti of Dar-ul-Ifta Ahl-e-Sunnat, Mufti Muhammad Abdul Majid al-Attari al-Madani.

May Allah Almighty accept this effort of ours and make it beneficial for people, especially the students.

اٰمِيْن بِجَاهِ النَّبِيِّ الْاَمِيْن صَلَّى اللّٰهُ عَلَيْهِ وَاٰلِهٖ وَسَلَّم

Department "Seerat-e-Mustafa" (Islamic Research Centre)

Sha'ban al-Mu'azzam 1442 AH/March 2021

Chapter 1

Blessed Birth of the Beloved Prophet صَلَّى اللهُ عَلَيْهِ وَسَلَّم

Excellence of Salat upon the Prophet ﷺ

The Final Messenger of Allah صَلَّى اللهُ عَلَيْهِ وَاٰلِهٖ وَسَلَّم has stated:

لَا تَجْعَلُوا بُیُوتَکُمْ قُبُوْرًا وَلَا تَجْعَلُوا قَبْرِی عِیدًا وَصَلُّوا عَلَیَّ فَإِنَّ صَلَاتَکُمْ تَبْلُغُنِی حَیْثُ کُنْتُمْ

'Do not make your homes a graveyard nor make my grave an Eid, and recite Salat upon me. Indeed, your Salat reaches me wherever you are.'[1]

Darkness of Ignorance

The basic purpose of the creation of humans is to worship Allah Almighty and obey Him, but humans become oblivious of this purpose due to the glitter of this world and the deception of *Nafs* and Satan. In order to remind humans of this purpose and guide them to the right path, Allah عَزَّوَجَلَّ sent many prophets in different ages. The blessed prophets would make people recognize their real purpose and guide them. These prophets were sent to specific nations and countries in different ages. At the end, Allah عَزَّوَجَلَّ sent

1 Abu Dawood, vol. 2, p. 315, Hadith 2042

the Holy Prophet صَلَّى اللهُ عَلَيْهِ وَاٰلِهٖ وَسَلَّم as a Prophet to the whole universe until the Day of Judgement.

The teachings of the previous prophets were forgotten before his advent. The entire world was lost in the darkness of ignorance. Many evils had engulfed all the societies of the world. The Arabian Peninsula, in particular, was in an extremely terrible state. Cruelty and injustice, immodesty and obscenity, quarrelling, gambling and excessive consumption of alcohol, massacre, ignorant customs, idolatry, and arrogance had caused the darkness of ignorance to spread all around.

Blessings of the Birth of the Prophet صَلَّى اللهُ عَلَيْهِ وَسَلَّم

Under such circumstances, the Final Messenger of Allah صَلَّى اللهُ عَلَيْهِ وَاٰلِهٖ وَسَلَّم was born. Certain events occurred with his blessed birth which served as a glad tiding, indicating that now, such an era has arrived in which the light of Islam will eliminate the darkness of disbelief.

The palace of Nausherwaan being struck by an earthquake, causing its fourteen spikes to collapse; the sudden extinguishing of the rising flames which had been continuously blazing for centuries at the worship place of the fire worshippers in Iran; the fast flowing "River Sava" drying up; these events and many more similar events were indications that a revolutionary change had now taken place and a new era had begun.

The Birth of the Prophet Enlightened the World

Under such circumstances, the rays of honour and joy shone in the seemingly simple house of Sayyidatuna Aaminah رَضِیَ اللہُ عَنْهَا, and the Holy Prophet صَلَّی اللہُ عَلَیْہِ وَاٰلِہٖ وَسَلَّم was born. Not only was his mother happy at his blessed birth, but it brought happiness to all grieved and afflicted people too.

He صَلَّی اللہُ عَلَیْہِ وَاٰلِہٖ وَسَلَّم belonged to Banu Hashim, a branch of Quraysh, the famous Arab tribe. His family is the most superior of all families. The Final Messenger of Allah صَلَّی اللہُ عَلَیْہِ وَاٰلِہٖ وَسَلَّم has said himself: "Allah Almighty made 'Kinanah' noble from amongst the progeny of Sayyiduna Ismail عَلَیْہِ السَّلَام, and chose Quraish from amongst 'Kinanah', and chose 'Banu Hashim' from amongst 'Quraysh', and chose me from amongst 'Banu Hashim'."[1]

According to a famous opinion, he صَلَّی اللہُ عَلَیْہِ وَاٰلِہٖ وَسَلَّم was born 55 days after the incident of *As-hab al-Feel* on Monday 12th Rabi' al-Awwal, corresponding to 20th April 571 C.E, during the refulgent moments of dawn, when the darkness of night was departing and daylight was spreading, at his mother's house in Makkah *al-Mukarramah*[2].[3]

---

1 Muslim, p. 962, Hadith 5938

2 The full name of Makkah is Makkah al-Mukarramah. It is one of the most important and ancient cities of the world. The Qiblah of all the Muslims, the sacred Ka'bah, which was constructed by Sayyiduna Ibraheem عَلَیْہِ السَّلَام and his son, Sayyiduna Ismail عَلَیْہِ السَّلَام, is situated there. Now, the size of this city is 760 square kilometres. This city is located at the distance of approximately 80 miles from the sea and 277 metres above sea level. The climate of this city is comparatively hot. In summer, it is very hot and the temperature usually rises to 40 °C. The Final Messenger of Allah صَلَّی اللہُ عَلَیْہِ وَاٰلِہٖ وَسَلَّم spent around 53 years of his blessed apparent life here.

3 Madarij al-Nubuwwah, section 1, vol. 2, p. 14, selected

Lineage *of the* Prophet

His blessed lineage from the side of his father is as follows:

1. Sayyiduna Muhammad ﷺ
2. the son of Abdullah
3. the son of Abdul Muttalib
4. the son of Hashim
5. the son of Abd Manaaf
6. the son of Qusay
7. the son of Kilaab
8. the son of Murrah
9. the son of Ka'b
10. the son of Lu`ai
11. the son of Ghalib
12. the son of Fihar
13. the son of Malik
14. the son of Nadar
15. the son of Kinanah
16. the son of Khuzaymah
17. the son of Mudrikah
18. the son of Ilyas
19. the son of Mudar
20. the son of Nizaar
21. the son of Ma'd
22. the son of Adnan.[1]

His blessed lineage from the side of his mother is as follows:

1. Sayyiduna Muhammad صَلَّى اللهُ عَلَيْهِ وَاٰلِهٖ وَسَلَّم
2. the son of Aaminah
3. the daughter of Wahb
4. the son of Abd Manaaf
5. the son of Zuhrah
6. the son of Kilaab.[2]

1 Al-Seerat-un-Nabawiyyah by Ibn-e-Hishaam, vol. 1, p. 89-103, summarised

2 Al-Seerat-un-Nabawiyyah by Ibn-e-Hishaam, vol. 1, p. 238, summarised

PARENTS *of the* PROPHET

His father was Sayyiduna Abdullah رَضِیَ اللّٰہُ عَنۡہُ, who was matchless in appearance as well as character. He passed away before the blessed birth of the Prophet صَلَّى اللّٰهُ عَلَيۡهِ وَاٰلِهٖ وَسَلَّم at the age of 25.[1]

His mother was Sayyidatuna Aaminah رَضِیَ اللّٰہُ عَنۡہَا. In regards to lineage and nobility, she was the most superior amongst the women of Quraysh. After the blessed passing of his father, she رَضِیَ اللّٰہُ عَنۡہَا brought up her beloved son.

1 Al-Seerat-un-Nabawiyyah by-Ibn-e-Hishaam, vol. 1, p. 89-103, summarised

Chapter 2

The Blessed Early Childhood *of the* Beloved Prophet ﷺ

The Suckling Period

It was the custom of the nobles of Makkah that instead of keeping their children with their mothers, they would send them to tribes living in rural areas to spend their childhood. It was because they wanted their children to eat pure food so that their organs and bodies could become strong, and so they could also converse eloquently in Arabic like them after learning the purest form of Arabic from them.

For this reason, the Beloved Prophet صَلَّى اللّٰهُ عَلَيْهِ وَاٰلِهٖ وَسَلَّم was handed over to Sayyidatuna Haleemah Sa'diyyah رَضِیَ اللّٰهُ عَنْهَا. She belonged to the Banu Sa'd tribe[1], which was a branch of Bani Hawazin. This tribe was second to none in eloquence and standard of Arabic. Sayyidatuna Haleemah

1 Banu Sa'd is situated at the distance of 15 to 20 kilometres from a village named Shuqsaan, that is located on the way from Makkah to Ta'if. This area is not completely barren. Cultivation is possible at some places. The climate and weather of this area is very good for health. The name of the village of Sayyidatuna Haleemah is 'Shawhatah'. It is also called 'Shuhtah'. It is at a distance of around 153 kilometres from Makkah by road.

رَضِیَ اللّٰہُ عَنْہَا came to Makkah with the women of her tribe to take a child to suckle. The fortune of Sayyidatuna Haleemah رَضِیَ اللّٰہُ عَنْہَا was at its peak that she was privileged to suckle the Prophet صَلَّى اللّٰهُ عَلَيْهِ وَاٰلِهٖ وَسَلَّم for two years.[1]

Blessing of Suckling

According to some narrations, in addition to Sayyidah Haleemah رَضِیَ اللّٰہُ عَنْہَا, six other fortunate women also had the privilege to suckle the Beloved Prophet صَلَّى اللّٰهُ عَلَيْهِ وَاٰلِهٖ وَسَلَّم. All these women were blessed with the treasure of faith.[2]

The reward earned by Sayyidah Haleemah رَضِیَ اللّٰہُ عَنْہَا for suckling the Holy Prophet صَلَّى اللّٰهُ عَلَيْهِ وَاٰلِهٖ وَسَلَّم was that her entire household was enriched with the treasure of faith.

Her husband is Sayyiduna Harith رَضِیَ اللّٰہُ عَنْہُ,[3] their son is Abdullah Bin Harith رَضِیَ اللّٰہُ عَنْہُ, and their two daughters are Unaysah Bint Harith and Judamah Bint Harith رَضِیَ اللّٰہُ عَنْہُمَا. It is Judamah Bint Harith, also famously known as Shayma, who was the elder milk-sister of the Final Messenger of Allah صَلَّى اللّٰهُ عَلَيْهِ وَاٰلِهٖ وَسَلَّم. She would comfort him in her arms and soothe him with lullabies.[4]

---

1 Derived from Sharh Zurqaani Aai-al-Mawahib, vol. 1, p. 278

2 Seerat Halabiyyah, vol. 1, p. 124 summarised

3 He was a believer, and attained blessings from the blessed company of the Final Messenger of Allah ﷺ. Moreover, he also presented himself in the Prophetic court. *(Fatawa Razawiyyah, vol. 30, p. 293)*

4 Tabaqaat Ibn Sa'd, vol. 1, p. 89

Childhood *Events and* Blessings

When Sayyidatuna Haleemah Sa'diyyah رَضِیَ اللّٰہُ عَنۡہَا reached the blessed house of the Final Messenger of Allah صَلَّى اللهُ عَلَيْهِ وَاٰلِهٖ وَسَلَّم to take him, she said: "I saw that the Beloved Prophet صَلَّى اللهُ عَلَيْهِ وَاٰلِهٖ وَسَلَّم was wrapped in a white cloth; fragrance was emanating from him; a green silk cloth was spread beneath him and he was resting on his blessed back. When I went near him slowly, picked him up and placed my hand on his blessed chest, he started smiling. He opened his naturally kohl-filled eyes and started looking at me. I felt that light was emanating from his eyes and reaching the sky. I spontaneously kissed him between both of his eyes and embraced him."[1]

When she رَضِیَ اللّٰہُ عَنۡہَا sat down to suckle him, the blessings of Prophethood started appearing. Glory be to Allah عَزَّوَجَلَّ! Her milk increased so much that the Beloved Prophet صَلَّى اللهُ عَلَيْهِ وَاٰلِهٖ وَسَلَّم and his milk-brother, Abdullah bin Harith, suckled to their fill and both slept peacefully.

1 Madarij-un-Nubuwwah, vol. 2, p. 19, summarised

The Beloved Prophet صَلَّى اللهُ عَلَيْهِ وَاٰلِهٖ وَسَلَّم would suckle from only one side of his milk-mother; he would not suckle from the other side even if she wanted to suckle him from the other side, as it was the share of his milk-brother. This indicated that the Beloved Prophet صَلَّى اللهُ عَلَيْهِ وَاٰلِهٖ وَسَلَّم would promote justice.

By virtue of his blessing, the she-camel of Sayyidatuna Haleemah رَضِىَ اللهُ عَنْهَا, which was weak and did not have milk, developed plenty of milk. The husband of Sayyidatuna Haleemah milked the she-camel and they both drank its milk to their fill. They spent the night with great comfort and peace, and slept very well for the whole night.

When they woke up, Harith Bin Abd al-'Uzza, the husband of Sayyidatuna Haleemah رَضِىَ اللهُ عَنْهَا, said: "Haleemah, you have brought a very blessed child." Sayyidatuna Haleemah رَضِىَ اللهُ عَنْهَا replied: "I also hope that this child is very blessed and he has come to us as a mercy of Allah. Very soon, our home will be filled with goodness and blessings."[1]

Sayyidah Haleemah رَضِىَ اللهُ عَنْهَا states: "(When) we left for our village from Makkah with the Holy Prophet صَلَّى اللهُ عَلَيْهِ وَاٰلِهٖ وَسَلَّم, my mule which had remained behind the entire caravan on the way due to weakness started to walk so fast that no other riding animal could compete with it."[2]

1 Seerat-e-Halbiyyah, vol. 1, p. 32, summarised
2 Madarij-un-Nubuwwah, vol. 2, p. 20, summarised

Some Beautiful Aspects of his Childhood

When the Final Messenger of Allah صَلَّى اللّٰهُ عَلَيْهِ وَاٰلِهٖ وَسَلَّم came to Sayyidah Haleemah Sa'diyyah رَضِیَ اللّٰهُ عَنْهَا, her animals started increasing in number, her dignity increased, and she started to attain goodness and blessings.

As long as the Beloved Prophet صَلَّى اللّٰهُ عَلَيْهِ وَاٰلِهٖ وَسَلَّم remained there, the house of Sayyidah Haleemah رَضِیَ اللّٰهُ عَنْهَا remained filled with goodness and blessings. These blessings continued to increase day by day and the members of the household started living a prosperous life.

Sayyidah Haleemah رَضِیَ اللّٰهُ عَنْهَا states: "I was very comfortable while looking after him when he was at the age of suckling. He would neither scream nor cry like other children.

He started crawling at the age of 2 months, standing up at the age of 3 months, walking in every direction with the support of a wall at the age of 4 months, and he was able to walk properly at the age of 5 months. At the age of 8 months, he would speak in a way that could be understood clearly; and at the age of 9 months, he started to speak eloquently."[1]

Sayyidah Haleemah رَضِیَ اللّٰهُ عَنْهَا has further added: "The sentence that he spoke at the early age was اَللّٰهُ اَكْبَرُ كَبِيْرًا وَّالْحَمْدُ لِلّٰهِ كَثِيْرًا (Translation: Allah is the greatest, and every type of praise is for Allah Almighty). Whilst in his cradle, he would talk to the moon, and it would bow down in whichever direction he would point."[2]

---

1 Madarij an-Nubuwwah, vol.2, pg. 20
2 Jam'-ul-Jawami', vol. 3, p. 212, Hadith 8361

Blessings of the Presence of the Prophet

Sayyidah Haleemah رَضِیَ اللہُ عَنْہَا mentions the blessings of the Beloved Prophet صَلَّى اللّٰهُ عَلَيْهِ وَاٰلِهٖ وَسَلَّم in the following manner:

- My tribe, Bani Sa'd, was suffering from a drought. When I reached my tribe with him, the drought finished. The land became lush green, trees became filled with fruit and animals became very healthy.
- One day, my neighbour said to me: "O Haleemah! Your home remains bright throughout the night. What is the reason?" I replied: "This light is not due to any lamp, but due to the luminous face of (Prophet) Muhammad صَلَّى اللّٰهُ عَلَيْهِ وَاٰلِهٖ وَسَلَّم."
- I had seven goats. When I moved his blessed hand over the goats, by virtue of his blessing, the goats started to give milk so much that the milk of one day would suffice for 40 days. Not only that, my goats also received such blessings that they rose to 700 in number from only 7.
- My tribe once said to me: "Give us some share as well from his blessings!" Thus, I put his blessed feet in a pond of water, and made the goats of the tribe drink that water. Thereby, their goats gave birth to kids and their milk made the tribe prosperous and wealthy.
- When children would call him to play, he would say: "I have not been created for playing."
- He would go to the countryside with my children where the goats would graze. One day, my son said to me: "Dear mother! (Prophet) Muhammad صَلَّى اللّٰهُ عَلَيْهِ وَاٰلِهٖ وَسَلَّم holds immense grandeur. Whichever field he goes to, it becomes lush green; a cloud shades him in the sun; his foot does not leave any impression

on sand; stones become soft like dough under his feet, leaving footprints on them; (and) the animals of the countryside kiss his blessed feet."[1]

Duration of Stay in Banu Sa'd and Return

Sayyidah Haleemah رَضِیَ اللّٰہُ عَنْہَا and her family continued to observe the blessings from the Final Messenger of Allah صَلَّی اللّٰہُ عَلَیْہِ وَاٰلِہٖ وَسَلَّم at every moment. They continued to gain spiritual blessings from him and shape their destiny by virtue of him.

Soon, two years passed by. Sayyidah Haleemah رَضِیَ اللّٰہُ عَنْہَا weaned him and took him to his mother, Sayyidatuna Aaminah رَضِیَ اللّٰہُ عَنْہَا, as per agreement. Sayyidatuna Aaminah رَضِیَ اللّٰہُ عَنْہَا blessed Sayyidah Haleemah رَضِیَ اللّٰہُ عَنْہَا with gifts as per her (financial) ability. Seeing the blessings of the Beloved Prophet صَلَّی اللّٰہُ عَلَیْہِ وَاٰلِہٖ وَسَلَّم, Sayyidah Haleemah strongly desired for him to spend more time with her in her tribe.

What a coincidence it was that during the same days, there was an outbreak of an epidemic in Makkah. Sayyidah Haleemah رَضِیَ اللّٰہُ عَنْہَا convinced Sayyidatuna Aaminah رَضِیَ اللّٰہُ عَنْہَا to send the Beloved Prophet صَلَّی اللّٰہُ عَلَیْہِ وَاٰلِہٖ وَسَلَّم to her tribe for some more time so that he could stay safe from the epidemic disease.

In this way, Sayyidah Haleema's رَضِیَ اللّٰہُ عَنْہَا heartfelt desire was fulfilled, her house was once again illuminated with the beloved of Sayyidatuna Aaminah رَضِیَ اللّٰہُ عَنْہَا, and her house once again became the centre of mercies and blessings by the virtue of the blessed presence of the Beloved Prophet صَلَّی اللّٰہُ عَلَیْہِ وَاٰلِہٖ وَسَلَّم.

He صَلَّی اللّٰہُ عَلَیْہِ وَاٰلِہٖ وَسَلَّم remained in the Banu Sa'd tribe for approximately four years. He took goats to graze with his milk-siblings as well

1 Al-Kalaam al-Awdah fi Tafseer Alam Nashrah (Anwar-e-Jamal-e-Mustafa), p. 107-109, summarised

over there. To look after goats after taking them to the pastures is the Sunnah of almost all the prophets عَلَيْهِمُ الصَّلٰوةُ وَالسَّلَام. He صَلَّى اللهُ عَلَيْهِ وَاٰلِهٖ وَسَلَّم revealed one of his Prophetic traits in his childhood through this action of his.

When the first [event of] *Shaqq al-Sadr* occurred in the tribe of Banu Sa'd, it worried Sayyidah Haleemah رَضِىَ اللهُ عَنْهَا, and she brought him to Sayyidatuna Aaminah رَضِىَ اللهُ عَنْهَا, handing him over to her. After this, he صَلَّى اللهُ عَلَيْهِ وَاٰلِهٖ وَسَلَّم was brought up by his beloved mother.

Shaqq al-Sadr means the splitting of the chest. The angels split the blessed chest of the Final Messenger of Allah صَلَّى اللهُ عَلَيْهِ وَاٰلِهٖ وَسَلَّم, took out his blessed heart and washed it. This act is called *Shaqq al-Sadr*. This act was carried out four times in his blessed life. The first time it was carried out was when he was four years old, the second time when he was ten years old, the third time when he was 40 years old, and the fourth time before going to the journey of *Mi'raj*. It is famous that this valley of Banu Sa'd (pictured) is where the splitting of the chest occurred.

Chapter 3

The Blessed Late Childhood *of the* Beloved Prophet ﷺ

The Sorrowful Passing *of* His Beloved Mother

When the Final Messenger of Allah صَلَّى اللهُ عَلَيْهِ وَاٰلِهٖ وَسَلَّم was six years old, his blessed mother took him to Madinah to visit his father's maternal family. Sayyidatuna Umm Ayman رَضِیَ اللهُ عَنْهَا was also accompanying them in this journey. She was the maidservant of his father.

Upon return, the Beloved Prophet's صَلَّى اللهُ عَلَيْهِ وَاٰلِهٖ وَسَلَّم mother passed away at Abwa[1], and was buried at the same place. His father had already passed away, and now, his mother had passed away too. Sayyidatuna Umm Ayman رَضِیَ اللهُ عَنْهَا wiped his tears, consoled him, took him back to Makkah, and handed him over to his grandfather, Sayyiduna Abdul Muttalib رَضِیَ اللهُ عَنْه.

---

1 Abwa is a valley that is situated between Makkah and Madinah in the direction of the sea. It is at a distance of almost 261 kilometres from Makkah, and 222 kilometres from Madinah. One Ghazwa also took place in the Abwa Valley in which no fighting took place. Nowadays, the Abwa Valley is known as Khuraibah.

After the Passing of his Parents

After the passing of his parents, the Beloved Prophet صَلَّى اللّٰهُ عَلَيْهِ وَاٰلِهٖ وَسَلَّم was brought up by his grandfather whose name was Abdul Muttalib رَضِیَ اللّٰهُ عَنْهُ. He was the chief of Makkah. He loved his blessed grandson greatly; he would keep him with himself at all time, he would make him sit with him, he would feed him with himself, and he would put him to sleep by his side at night.

A special chair would be placed in the courtyard around the *Ka'bah* for Abdul Muttalib to sit upon. Even influential dignitaries did not possess the courage to step on it, but when the Final Messenger of Allah صَلَّى اللّٰهُ عَلَيْهِ وَاٰلِهٖ وَسَلَّم would come, he would move forward without any hesitation to sit on the seat of his grandfather.[1] Then when he was eight years old, his grandfather also passed away.[2]

After this, he was brought up by his uncle, Abu Taalib. Regarding his blessed childhood, Abu Taalib states: "I never saw that the Beloved Prophet صَلَّى اللّٰهُ عَلَيْهِ وَاٰلِهٖ وَسَلَّم ever told a lie, deceived anyone, harmed anyone, went to play with indecent children, or ever spoke unsophisticatedly. He was always the possessor of formidable demeanour, noble traits, exalted character, and he was always very soft-spoken, extremely pious, and chaste to the highest degree."[3]

1 Al-Seerat-un-Nabawiyyah, vol. 1, p. 306
2 Sharah Al-Zurqani Ala al-Mawahib, vol. 1, p. 306
3 Seerat-e-Mustafa, p. 83

Further Blessings of Childhood

At the age of 8, when his uncle Abu Taalib took the responsibility of custodianship. He too received a downpour of goodness and blessings. He would love him more than his own children, and would not let him go out of his sight.

Abu Taalib states: "Whenever my children would eat food (before the Beloved Prophet صَلَّى اللهُ عَلَيْهِ وَاٰلِهٖ وَسَلَّم), they would not satisfy their hunger, but since the Holy Prophet صَلَّى اللهُ عَلَيْهِ وَاٰلِهٖ وَسَلَّم started eating food with them, all the children would be satiated. Therefore, whenever I wanted to give food to my children, I would say: "Stop! Let my son (Muhammad صَلَّى اللهُ عَلَيْهِ وَاٰلِهٖ وَسَلَّم) arrive, then start eating."

Similarly, whenever he wanted to give milk to his children, he would first give it to the Beloved Prophet صَلَّى اللهُ عَلَيْهِ وَاٰلِهٖ وَسَلَّم, and then to his children (and there would be enough for all of them). If any of his sons would drink the milk first, all the milk would be finished by that single child. Seeing this, Abu Taalib would say: "O Muhammad صَلَّى اللهُ عَلَيْهِ وَاٰلِهٖ وَسَلَّم! What can be said about your blessings!"[1]

Journey to Yemen

When the Beloved Prophet صَلَّى اللهُ عَلَيْهِ وَاٰلِهٖ وَسَلَّم was 10 years old, he went to Yemen with his uncle, Zubair. On the way, a very strange event took place.

A camel was preventing people from passing by in a valley. When the camel saw the Beloved Prophet صَلَّى اللهُ عَلَيْهِ وَاٰلِهٖ وَسَلَّم, it sat down and

1 Dalaa`il-un-Nubuwwah, vol. 1, p. 95

started rubbing its chest against the ground. The Beloved Prophet صَلَّى اللهُ عَلَيْهِ وَاٰلِهٖ وَسَلَّم dismounted his own camel and mounted it. When he صَلَّى اللهُ عَلَيْهِ وَاٰلِهٖ وَسَلَّم reached the other side of the valley, he left the camel.

Upon returning from the journey, he صَلَّى اللهُ عَلَيْهِ وَاٰلِهٖ وَسَلَّم saw that the valley had been flooded with water. He صَلَّى اللهُ عَلَيْهِ وَاٰلِهٖ وَسَلَّم asked the Quraysh to follow him. He صَلَّى اللهُ عَلَيْهِ وَاٰلِهٖ وَسَلَّم entered the valley and all the Quraysh followed him. Allah Almighty made the water dry up. When the people returned to Makkah, they related this event to everyone. Having heard this, they said that the eminent sublimity of this child is matchless.[1]

First Business Trip *to the* Levant (Shaam)

When the Beloved Prophet صَلَّى اللهُ عَلَيْهِ وَاٰلِهٖ وَسَلَّم was 12 years old, he made his first business trip to the Levant

1 Subul al-Huda War-Rashad, vol. 2, p. 139

with his uncle, Abu Taalib. When the caravan reached the city of Busraa, he met a monk called Baheera, whose real name was '**Barjees**'. He recognized the Beloved Prophet صَلَّى اللّٰهُ عَلَيْهِ وَاٰلِهٖ وَسَلَّم by the signs of prophethood. Holding his hand, he made the following announcement: "He is the chief of all the worlds; he is the Messenger of the Lord of the worlds; Allah Almighty will send him as رحمةً للعالمين (mercy for all the worlds)."

He then arranged a meal for the Beloved Prophet صَلَّى اللّٰهُ عَلَيْهِ وَاٰلِهٖ وَسَلَّم and the people of the caravan. He saw some more signs of Prophethood during the meal. He said to Abu Taalib: "Do not take him to the Levant. If the people of the Levant recognize him by the signs of Prophethood, they will try to assassinate him."

Therefore, he returned from there. That monk also gave him some provisions for the journey.[1]

FURTHER BUSINESS TRIPS

The Final Messenger of Allah صَلَّى اللّٰهُ عَلَيْهِ وَاٰلِهٖ وَسَلَّم went on many business trips. At the age of 10, he went on a business trip to Yemen with his uncle, Sayyiduna Zubair bin Abdul Muttalib رَضِىَ اللّٰهُ عَنْهُمَا.[2] Of the business trips he صَلَّى اللّٰهُ عَلَيْهِ وَاٰلِهٖ وَسَلَّم carried out for Sayyidatuna Khadija رَضِىَ اللّٰهُ عَنْهَا, two of them were also to Yemen[3].

It has been reported: "Sayyidatuna Khadija رَضِىَ اللّٰهُ عَنْهَا sent him twice to Jurash (a place in Yemen) for trade, and a she-camel was given for each of these two trips."[4]

1 Derived from Tirmizi, vol. 5, p. 356-357, Hadith 3640
2 Subul-al-Huda War-Rashad, vol. 2, p. 139
3 The distance between Yemen and Makkah is approximately 1,034 Kilometres.
4 Mustadrak, vol. 4, p. 178, Hadith 4887

Participation in 'Hilf-ul-Fudool'

A person from the city of Zubayd came to Makkah to sell his goods. A person named 'Aas bin Waa`il bought goods from him, but did not make the payment. The trader requested for help from some of the tribes, but none of them helped him. He then climbed Mount Abi Qubays[1] and made a request for help to everyone. Upon this, some peace-loving people of Quraish launched a reform movement.

Prominent chiefs gathered at the house of Abdullah bin Jud'aan, where Sayyiduna Zubair Bin Abdul Muttalib رَضِیَ اللّٰہُ عَنْہُمَا, the uncle of the Beloved Prophet صَلَّى اللّٰهُ عَلَيْهِ وَاٰلِهٖ وَسَلَّم, suggested that they should make a mutual agreement. The chiefs of Quraysh entered into an agreement and made a firm intention that they would eradicate unrest, protect travellers, help the poor, support the oppressed and hold cruel people to account.

The Holy Prophet صَلَّى اللّٰهُ عَلَيْهِ وَاٰلِهٖ وَسَلَّم also participated in this agreement. Even after the declaration of prophethood, the Beloved Prophet صَلَّى اللّٰهُ عَلَيْهِ وَاٰلِهٖ وَسَلَّم would express joy upon participating in this agreement, and would say: "I was so pleased due to this agreement that if someone had given me red camels in return of this agreement, I would not have felt as pleased. Even today, if an oppressed person calls me for help under this agreement, I am ready to help him."[2]

This agreement has been named 'Hilf-ul-Fudool'. The reason behind

---

1 Abu Qubays is a mountain which is located outside Masjid al-Haraam near Safa and Marwa. By the Divine command, this was the first mountain to be created in the world. This mountain is also called 'Al-Ameen'. (Tafsir ad-Durr al-Manthur, vol 2, pg. 266, Balad al-Amin, pg. 206)

2 Al-Raud-ul-Unuf, vol. 1, p. 242-244

this is that a long time ago, an agreement was made in Makkah. The names of all those who caused this agreement to be formed were 'Fadl'. For this reason, it was named 'Hilf-ul-Fudool', i.e. the agreement made by the few people whose names were 'Fadl'.[1]

1 Seerat-un-Nabawiyyah by Ibn-e-Hishaam, vol. 1, p. 265

Chapter 4

Blessed Youth *of the* Beloved Prophet ﷺ

Second Business Trip to the Levant

The Final Messenger of Allah صَلَّى اللّٰهُ عَلَيْهِ وَاٰلِهٖ وَسَلَّم possessed a sublime character from the beginning. When he reached the age of 25, his truthfulness and honesty became acclaimed everywhere. He became famous as "**Sadiq**" (the truthful) and "**Ameen**" (the trustworthy) all around Makkah.

There was an esteemed and wealthy noblewoman of Makkah, named "Khadija". She needed an honest person who could take her trade goods to the Levant for sale and return with a profit for her.

When the acclaim of his trustworthiness and truthfulness reached her, she sent him a message, saying: "Take my trade goods to the Levant. I will pay you double the amount that I pay others."

The Holy Prophet صَلَّى اللّٰهُ عَلَيْهِ وَاٰلِهٖ وَسَلَّم accepted this request of hers and departed for the Levant with the trade goods. The slave of Sayyidatuna Khadija رَضِیَ اللّٰهُ عَنْهَا, named 'Maysarah', was also accompanying him in this trip who would serve him and fulfil his other needs.

Once again, when the Holy Prophet صَلَّى اللّٰهُ عَلَيْهِ وَاٰلِهٖ وَسَلَّم reached Busra, the famous city of the Levant, he صَلَّى اللّٰهُ عَلَيْهِ وَاٰلِهٖ وَسَلَّم rested near the place of worship of a monk named 'Nastoora'. That monk already knew Maysarah. Due to this, he came to him, and pointing towards the Prophet صَلَّى اللّٰهُ عَلَيْهِ وَاٰلِهٖ وَسَلَّم, asked him: "Who is that under this tree?" Maysarah replied: "He is a dweller of Makkah, and belongs to the Banu Hashim tribe; his name is '**Muhammad**' and his **title** is "**Ameen**".

The monk said: “No one except a prophet stopped under this tree.” He then asked: “Does redness remain in his eyes?”

Maysarah replied: “Yes, it does, and it remains all the time.”

Having heard this, Nastoora said: “He is the last Prophet of Allah Almighty. I can see all those signs in him which I read in the *Torah* and the *Zaboor*. I wish I could be alive when he (صَلَّى اللّٰهُ عَلَيْهِ وَاٰلِهٖ وَسَلَّم) declares his prophethood. If I stay alive, I will help him fully, and spend my entire life serving him. O Maysarah! I advise you not to ever leave him; keep serving him, because Allah Almighty has blessed him with prophethood.”

The Beloved Prophet صَلَّى اللّٰهُ عَلَيْهِ وَاٰلِهٖ وَسَلَّم returned soon after selling the trade goods. When his caravan reached Makkah, Sayyidatuna Khadija رَضِیَ اللّٰهُ عَنْهَا was sitting on her roof. She saw that two angels had shaded the Final Messenger of Allah صَلَّى اللّٰهُ عَلَيْهِ وَاٰلِهٖ وَسَلَّم from the sun. Observing this left a profound effect on Sayyidatuna Khadija رَضِیَ اللّٰهُ عَنْهَا.

After a few days, when she discussed this matter with her slave Maysarah, he told her that he witnessed such incidents throughout the journey. Maysarah then told her about the wondrous scenes he saw about the Beloved Prophet's صَلَّى اللّٰهُ عَلَيْهِ وَاٰلِهٖ وَسَلَّم truthfulness, honesty, treating others kindly, sympathising with them, understanding matters and business acumen. He also mentioned how Nastoora monk had wholeheartedly expressed his love for the Prophet صَلَّى اللّٰهُ عَلَيْهِ وَاٰلِهٖ وَسَلَّم and what he had predicted about him.

Having heard this, Sayyidatuna Khadija رَضِیَ اللّٰهُ عَنْهَا developed great reverence and devotion for the Beloved Prophet صَلَّى اللّٰهُ عَلَيْهِ وَاٰلِهٖ وَسَلَّم.

Marrying Sayyidatuna Khadija رَضِیَ اللّٰہُ عَنۡہَا

Sayyidatuna Khadija رَضِیَ اللّٰہُ عَنۡہَا was a wealthy and very respectable woman of Makkah. She belonged to Banu Asad Bin Abdul 'Uzaa, a branch of the Quraysh tribe. Three generations above, her lineage joins the lineage of the Beloved Prophet صَلَّى اللّٰہُ عَلَیۡہِ وَاٰلِہٖ وَسَلَّم.[1]

The people of Makkah would call her by the title 'Taahirah', i.e. 'the chaste one', due to her chastity. She was 40 years old at that time. She had married twice and both her husbands had passed away. Very rich and affluent people sent her marriage proposals, but she turned them down and had decided not to get married again.

However, after hearing about the Beloved Prophet's صَلَّى اللّٰہُ عَلَیۡہِ وَاٰلِہٖ وَسَلَّم sublime character, habits, blessings and astonishing events, her heart was inclined towards marrying him. She called the (paternal) aunt of the Final Messenger of Allah صَلَّى اللّٰہُ عَلَیۡہِ وَاٰلِہٖ وَسَلَّم, Sayyidatuna Safiyyah

1 Faizan-e-Khadija-tul-Kubra, p. 35-38

رَضِیَ اللّٰہُ عَنۡہَا, who was the wife of Awam Bin Khuwaylid, the brother of Sayyidatuna Khadija رَضِیَ اللّٰہُ عَنۡہَا.

Sayyidatuna Khadija رَضِیَ اللّٰہُ عَنۡہَا called Sayyidatuna Safiyyah رَضِیَ اللّٰہُ عَنۡہَا and sought some information regarding the personal details of the Beloved Prophet صَلَّى اللّٰهُ عَلَيْهِ وَاٰلِهٖ وَسَلَّم. Then, almost 3 months after returning from the journey of the Levant, she sent him a marriage proposal.

Sayyidatuna Khadija رَضِیَ اللّٰہُ عَنۡہَا herself mentioned the reason for liking him in this way: "I liked him because of his noble character and truthfulness."

The Beloved Prophet صَلَّى اللّٰهُ عَلَيْهِ وَاٰلِهٖ وَسَلَّم mentioned this marriage proposal to the elders of his family and uncles (younger brothers of his father). They accepted the marriage proposal. The Beloved Prophet's صَلَّى اللّٰهُ عَلَيْهِ وَاٰلِهٖ وَسَلَّم *Nikah* was performed in which his uncle, Abu Taalib, delivered the *Khutbah* and fixed a *Haq Mahr* of 20 camels from his own wealth.[1]

Sayyidatuna Khadija رَضِیَ اللّٰہُ عَنۡہَا remained in the servitude of the Beloved Prophet صَلَّى اللّٰهُ عَلَيْهِ وَاٰلِهٖ وَسَلَّم for almost 25 years. He صَلَّى اللّٰهُ عَلَيْهِ وَاٰلِهٖ وَسَلَّم did not marry any other woman during her life. Except for one son of the Holy Prophet صَلَّى اللّٰهُ عَلَيْهِ وَاٰلِهٖ وَسَلَّم, Sayyiduna Ibrahim رَضِیَ اللّٰہُ عَنۡہُ, all his other children were born to Sayyidatuna Khadija رَضِیَ اللّٰہُ عَنۡہَا. Sayyidatuna Khadija رَضِیَ اللّٰہُ عَنۡہَا sacrificed all her wealth for the Beloved Prophet صَلَّى اللّٰهُ عَلَيْهِ وَاٰلِهٖ وَسَلَّم, and spent her entire life under his servitude.

Role in the Construction of the Ka'bah

When the Final Messenger of Allah صَلَّى اللّٰهُ عَلَيْهِ وَاٰلِهٖ وَسَلَّم reached the age of 35, a torrential rain caused floodwater to enter the sanctuary of the *Ka'bah*, causing great damage to its building, resulting in some part of it to collapse. The Quraysh decided to reconstruct a strong building of the *Ka'bah* after demolishing the

1 Sharh al-Zurqaani 'ala al-Mawahib, vol. 1, p. 370 – 376, summarised

entire structure with an elevated door and also a roof.[1]

Therefore, the Quraysh started this construction work collectively. The Beloved Prophet صَلَّى اللهُ عَلَيْهِ وَاٰلِهٖ وَسَلَّم also participated in this construction and brought stones for it.

Different tribes divided different parts of the building of the *Ka'bah* between themselves, but when the time for placing *Hajar al-Aswad* arrived, differences arose. The tribes showed bitter disagreements with each other.

These are the images of Hajar al-Aswad. Hajar al-Aswad is a stone which was sent down from Paradise with Sayyiduna Adam عَلَيْهِ السَّلَام. To touch and kiss this stone erases sins. The Arabs considered this stone to be extremely sacred. This stone is embedded in the wall of the Ka'bah even today.

1 Seerat al-Halbiyyah, vol. 1, p. 204, briefly

Every tribe wanted to have the honour of placing the *Hajar al-Aswad*, and (their approach was such that) if any tribe becomes an obstacle in it, then it should be stopped by the force of the sword.

Four days were spent discussing as to who would place the *Hajar al-Aswad*. In order to prevent this discord, an elderly person made the following suggestion: "We will get the first person who enters the sanctuary tomorrow morning to decide this case for us. Whatever decision he makes, all the tribes will accept it." All the tribes agreed on this.

Glory be to Allah عَزَّوَجَلَّ! The person who first entered the sanctuary in the morning was the Beloved Prophet صَلَّى اللّٰهُ عَلَيْهِ وَاٰلِهٖ وَسَلَّم. Seeing him, they all were overjoyed, and said: "He is *Ameen*; whatever decision he makes, we will accept it."

With great wisdom, the Beloved Prophet صَلَّى اللّٰهُ عَلَيْهِ وَاٰلِهٖ وَسَلَّم resolved this discord. He صَلَّى اللّٰهُ عَلَيْهِ وَاٰلِهٖ وَسَلَّم said: "The tribes that want to place *Hajar al-Aswad* should choose one chief each."

They chose their chiefs. He صَلَّى اللّٰهُ عَلَيْهِ وَاٰلِهٖ وَسَلَّم then spread his blessed shawl and placed *Hajar al-Aswad* on it and told the chiefs that they all should lift *Hajar al-Aswad* by holding the shawl.

Everyone did so, and when *Hajar al-Aswad* was taken near its place, the Beloved Prophet صَلَّى اللّٰهُ عَلَيْهِ وَاٰلِهٖ وَسَلَّم lifted the sacred stone and placed it at its place with his blessed hands. In this way, by virtue of his wisdom, the rising flames of discord and conflict were extinguished, bringing joy and happiness to everyone's heart.[1]

His Sublime Character so Far

The entire life of the Final Messenger of Allah صَلَّى اللّٰهُ عَلَيْهِ وَاٰلِهٖ وَسَلَّم was a paradigm of sublime character and noble habits even before the declaration of Prophethood. Whether it was veracity, honesty, loyalty, keeping promises, respecting elders, being affectionate towards the young, ones having sympathy for the weak, kindness,

1 Seerat al-Nabawiyyah, vol. 2, p. 13, summarised

generosity, well-wishing for others, mercifulness, or softness, he صَلَّى اللهُ عَلَيْهِ وَاٰلِهٖ وَسَلَّم was matchless and incomparable in every virtuous deed and noble habit. He صَلَّى اللهُ عَلَيْهِ وَاٰلِهٖ وَسَلَّم was free from every type of ill habit, like greed, deception, lying, breaking promises, drinking alcohol, dancing, singing, plundering, theft, obscene conversation, etc., which were very common in the era of ignorance [pre-Islamic era]. In fact, his eminent grandeur is such that even in the debased society of the Arabs of that time, his nobility, honesty, trustworthiness and truthfulness were highly acclaimed far and wide.

The people of Makkah had special reverence for him in their hearts due to his noble character. He reached the age of 40, but remained pure of all immoral, pagan and ignorant activities.

Idolatry was so common in Makkah that in the sacred *Ka'bah* alone, 360 idols were kept that were worshiped, but he صَلَّى اللهُ عَلَيْهِ وَاٰلِهٖ وَسَلَّم never bowed down before them.

It was the excellence of his previously spent life that after his declaration of Prophethood, his enemies tried their utmost to find even a minor flaw in any era of his life, or prove any weakness in his so-far-spent life so that they could tarnish the honour and dignity of the Holy Prophet صَلَّى اللهُ عَلَيْهِ وَاٰلِهٖ وَسَلَّم and prove him inferior before the people, but thousands of his enemies were rendered unsuccessful in this regard and could not bring forth even a single incident which they could use to point fingers at his sublime character.

Therefore, as soon as he declared his prophethood, fortunate individuals devoted themselves to him after reciting his *Kalimah*.

Chapter 5

Divine Revelation and the Stages *of the* Propagation *of* Islam

Worship *in the* Cave *of* Hira

When the Final Messenger of Allah صَلَّى اللّٰهُ عَلَيْهِ وَاٰلِهٖ وَسَلَّم reached the age of 40, a new transformation took place in him. The passion of Divine love and worshipping the Almighty took him to a cave, taking him out of the busy life of Makkah.

He صَلَّى اللّٰهُ عَلَيْهِ وَاٰلِهٖ وَسَلَّم would stay alone there and remain engrossed in the worship of Allah Almighty. Situated at a short distance from the blessed *Ka'bah*, he صَلَّى اللّٰهُ عَلَيْهِ وَاٰلِهٖ وَسَلَّم would go to the Cave of Hira with the food provisions of many days, and remain busy in worship and contemplation in the peaceful environment of the cave. When food would run out, he would sometimes come home himself to get it or at times, Sayyidatuna Khadija رَضِىَ اللّٰهُ عَنْهَا would send it there.

This luminous cave is still present in its original state today.

Beginning of Revelation *and the* Declaration *of* Prophethood

Revelation began with true dreams. Whatever dream the Beloved Prophet صَلَّى اللّٰهُ عَلَيْهِ وَاٰلِهٖ وَسَلَّم would have in his sleep at night, its interpretation would later become clear like the brightness of the day and the light of the sun.

Six months passed by in this state. In the blessed month of Ramadan, when he صَلَّى اللّٰهُ عَلَيْهِ وَاٰلِهٖ وَسَلَّم was in seclusion in the Cave of Hira, one night, Sayyiduna Jibraeel عَلَيْهِ السَّلَام, the chief of all angels, brought the first exalted message of Allah Almighty in the form of a revelation.[1]

1 Irshad-us-Saari, , vol. 1, p. 103, Under the Hadith 3

Then, the Divine revelation stopped for a while. After some time, he صَلَّى اللّٰهُ عَلَيْهِ وَاٰلِهٖ وَسَلَّم was going somewhere, and someone called him by addressing him as **'Ya Muhammad'**. When he looked at the sky, he found Sayyiduna Jibraeel عَلَيْهِ السَّلَام, who had come in the cave, now sitting on a chair between the earth and the sky.

He صَلَّى اللّٰهُ عَلَيْهِ وَاٰلِهٖ وَسَلَّم was overcome with fear; he went home and lay down, covering himself with a blanket. At that time, the following verses of the Quran were revealed:

يٰۤاَيُّهَا الْمُدَّثِّرُ ﴿۱﴾ قُمْ فَاَنْذِرْ ﴿۲﴾ وَ رَبَّكَ فَكَبِّرْ ﴿۳﴾ وَ ثِيَابَكَ فَطَهِّرْ ﴿۴﴾ وَ الرُّجْزَ فَاهْجُرْ ﴿۵﴾

O you who is enveloped in a cloak, (i.e. the Prophet Muhammad) Stand up and then warn. And proclaim the Purity of only your Lord. And keep your clothes pure. And keep away from the idols.[1]

The Cave of Hira is situated in Mount Noor which is at a distance of approximately 4 kilometres from *Masjid al-Haraam*. This cave is approximately more than 350 meters above the ground level. The special thing about this cave is that one can view the sacred *Ka'bah* directly from this cave. It is located at such an angle that the rays of the sun do not enter it. The cave is approximately 4 metres in length and 1.5 meters in width. The grandfather of the Holy Prophet صَلَّى اللّٰهُ عَلَيْهِ وَاٰلِهٖ وَسَلَّم, Sayyiduna Abdul Muttalib رَضِیَ اللّٰهُ عَنْهُ, would also come to this cave in the blessed month of Ramadan to perform worship. Even today, the fortunate devotees of the Prophet soothe their hearts and eyes by visiting this cave.

---

1 *[Kanz-ul-Iman (translation of Quran)]* *(Part 29, Al-Muddassir, Verses 1 to 5)*

Having received this command from His Lord, the Beloved Prophet صَلَّى اللهُ عَلَيْهِ وَاٰلِهٖ وَسَلَّم made a firm intention to raise the flag of truth and enlighten the world with the refulgence of monotheism [*tawheed*].[1]

Start of the Propagation of Islam and the First Stage

First of all, the Final Messenger of Allah صَلَّى اللهُ عَلَيْهِ وَاٰلِهٖ وَسَلَّم secretly invited those people to Islam whom he trusted and who were also acquainted with his circumstances. Under these circumstances, Sayyidatuna Khadija رَضِىَ اللهُ عَنْهَا was the first woman, Sayyiduna Abu Bakr رَضِىَ اللهُ عَنْهُ was the first free man, Sayyiduna Ali bin Abu Taalib رَضِىَ اللهُ عَنْهُ was the first boy, Sayyiduna Zaid Bin Harithah رَضِىَ اللهُ عَنْهُ was the first freed slave and Sayyiduna Bilal رَضِىَ اللهُ عَنْهُ was the first slave to embrace Islam.[2]

The propagation of Islam continued secretly. The way a thirsty person rushes towards fresh and cold water, in the same way, fortunate people rushed devotionally towards accepting the invitation of truth (Islam).

1 Bukhari, , vol. 1, p. 9, Hadith 4

2 Al-Mawahib-ul-ladunniyah, vol. 1, p. 115

A group of Muslims had been formed over the period of three years. During this period of time, he صَلَّى اللّٰهُ عَلَيْهِ وَاٰلِهٖ وَسَلَّم also stayed at *Dar al-Arqam*, where he would educate and guide the Muslims.[1]

Second stage of the Propagation of Islam

The following verse was then revealed after three years:

وَ اَنْذِرْ عَشِیْرَتَكَ الْاَقْرَبِیْنَ ﴿۲۱۴﴾

And, O Beloved, warn your closest relatives.[2]

In this blessed verse, the Beloved Prophet صَلَّى اللّٰهُ عَلَيْهِ وَاٰلِهٖ وَسَلَّم was commanded to also invite his close relatives to Islam. So, one day, he صَلَّى اللّٰهُ عَلَيْهِ وَاٰلِهٖ وَسَلَّم stood upon Mount Safa, and called the people of Quraysh. When all the people of the Quraysh tribe gathered, the Final Messenger of Allah صَلَّى اللّٰهُ عَلَيْهِ وَاٰلِهٖ وَسَلَّم said: "O my nation! If I say to you that an army is hiding behind this mountain which is about to attack you, will you believe me?"

All of them replied in one voice, saying: "Yes, definitely. We will believe you, because we have always found you truthful and trustworthy."

Then, the Beloved Prophet صَلَّى اللّٰهُ عَلَيْهِ وَاٰلِهٖ وَسَلَّم remarked: "I then say that I am warning you of the Divine torment, and if you do not embrace faith, then the torment of Allah Almighty will befall you."

---

1 Seerat-ul-Halbiyyah, vol. 1, p. 402

2 *[Kanz-ul-Iman (translation of Quran)] (Part 19, Surah Al-Shu'ara, Verse 214)*

Having heard this, all the people of Quraysh became displeased and left. His uncle, Abu Lahab, was also amongst them and he began to utter insolent words against the Beloved Prophet صَلَّى اللّٰهُ عَلَيْهِ وَاٰلِهٖ وَسَلَّم. The Beloved Prophet صَلَّى اللّٰهُ عَلَيْهِ وَاٰلِهٖ وَسَلَّم did not reply to his disrespect, but Allah Almighty revealed a complete Surah of the Holy Quran in condemnation of that evil blasphemer.[1]

The Third stage of the Propagation of Islam

In the fourth year of the declaration of Prophethood, the following verse of *Surah Hijr* was revealed:

فَاصْدَعْ بِمَا تُؤْمَرُ وَاَعْرِضْ عَنِ الْمُشْرِكِيْنَ ﴿٩٤﴾

Therefore, publicly announce what you are commanded, and turn away (your) face from the polytheists.[2]

In this blessed verse, Allah Almighty commanded His Beloved Prophet صَلَّى اللّٰهُ عَلَيْهِ وَاٰلِهٖ وَسَلَّم to propagate Islam openly to everyone. After this, he صَلَّى اللّٰهُ عَلَيْهِ وَاٰلِهٖ وَسَلَّم started propagating Islam and speaking against polytheism and idolatry openly. In this environment, the entire Quraysh, or rather the entire Arabian Peninsula, started opposing him.[3]

1 Bukhari, vol. 3, p. 294, Hadith 4770
2 *[Kanz-ul-Iman (translation of Quran)] (Part 14, Surah Al-Hijr, Verse 94)*
3 Sharh-ul-Zurqaani, vol. 1, p. 462

اللّٰهُ

Chapter 6

Oppressions of Disbelievers and

MIGRATION TO ABYSSINIA

Oppressions of Disbelievers upon the

BELOVED PROPHET ﷺ

As soon as the Beloved Prophet صَلَّى اللّٰهُ عَلَيْهِ وَاٰلِهٖ وَسَلَّم started propagating Islam openly, he was subjected to severe cruelty and oppression. Due to the expected revenge of Banu Hashim and the danger of having a war with them, the disbelievers could not martyr the Final Messenger of Allah صَلَّى اللّٰهُ عَلَيْهِ وَاٰلِهٖ وَسَلَّم, but they subjected him to oppression beyond any bound.

They would call him a foreteller, a sorcerer, mad and insane; they would utter insolent sentences against him, make taunting remarks, at times throw rubbish on him, at times pour blood of animals at his blessed door, at times put thorns on his way and at times, they would target his blessed body.

Once, when the Beloved Prophet صَلَّى اللّٰهُ عَلَيْهِ وَاٰلِهٖ وَسَلَّم was performing *Sajdah* in the sanctuary of the *Ka'bah*, a disbeliever named 'Uqbah, placed the intestines of a camel on his blessed back. Seeing this, the disbelievers started roaring with laughter. Then, Sayyidatuna Fatima رَضِیَ اللّٰهُ عَنْهَا came forward and removed it from him.[1]

Once, the Beloved Prophet صَلَّى اللّٰهُ عَلَيْهِ وَاٰلِهٖ وَسَلَّم was again offering *Salah* in the sanctuary of the *Ka'bah*. The disbeliever named Uqbah put a shawl around his neck and pulled it so hard that he صَلَّى اللّٰهُ عَلَيْهِ وَاٰلِهٖ وَسَلَّم began to feel strangled. Seeing this, Sayyiduna Abu Bakr Siddeeq رَضِیَ اللّٰهُ عَنْهُ moved forward and removed that disbeliever, pushing him away. Later on, the disbelievers tortured Sayyiduna Abu Bakr Siddeeq رَضِیَ اللّٰهُ عَنْهُ as well.[2]

---

1 Bukhari, vol. 1, p. 193, Hadith 520
2 Bukhari, vol. 2, p. 575, Hadith 3852

The Brutality of the **disbelievers** against the **Blessed Companions**

Along with the Final Messenger of Allah صَلَّى اللّٰهُ عَلَيْهِ وَاٰلِهٖ وَسَلَّم, the disbelievers crossed all limits in oppressing the honourable companions as well.

Once, Sayyiduna Abu Bakr Siddeeq رَضِیَ اللّٰہُ عَنْہُ started delivering a sermon in the sanctuary of the *Ka'bah*. Seeing this, the polytheists and disbelievers fiercely attacked the Muslims. They beat Sayyiduna Abu Bakr Siddeeq رَضِیَ اللّٰہُ عَنْہُ so much that his face was left covered with blood. His nose and ears were all covered in blood too, and his face could not be recognised. Sayyiduna Abu Bakr Siddeeq رَضِیَ اللّٰہُ عَنْہُ fell unconscious and remained unconscious for a long time.[1]

Sayyiduna Khabbaab رَضِیَ اللّٰہُ عَنْہُ embraced Islam at the time when only a few people had embraced Islam. Quraysh tortured him immensely. They tortured him to such an extent that once, they made him lie on his back on burning coals and one person stood on his chest. That person continued to stand on his chest until the burning coals were extinguished due to the flesh of his back melting. The marks of those coals remained on his back throughout his life. Once, Sayyiduna Umar al-Farooq رَضِیَ اللّٰہُ عَنْہُ saw those marks on his back during his caliphate. He رَضِیَ اللّٰہُ عَنْہُ became extremely sad and wept.[2]

1 Tareekh Ibn-e-Asakir, Raqm 3398, vol. 30, p. 49
2 Tabaqaat Ibn-e-Sa'd, Raqm 43, vol. 3, pp. 122 - 123

Sayyiduna Bilal رَضِیَ اللّٰہُ عَنْہُ would be dragged through the markets with his neck tied with a rope. He would be beaten relentlessly with sticks. In the scorching heat of the afternoon, he would be made to lie on scorching sand and a very heavy stone would be placed on his chest, resulting in his tongue coming out of his mouth. Even in this state, he would raise the slogan, 'Ahad Ahad'.[1]

Not only would men be tortured and oppressed, but the women who embraced Islam would also face hardships. Sayyidatuna Sumayyah رَضِیَ اللّٰہُ عَنْہَا, the mother of Sayyiduna Ammar bin Yasir رَضِیَ اللّٰہُ عَنْہُمَا, is that fortunate woman who was the first to sacrifice her life for Islam. She was an elderly woman, whom Abu Jahl martyred with a spear.[2]

She has the honour of becoming the first female martyr of Islam.

Migration *to* Abyssinia

When the disbelievers of Makkah did not refrain from causing harm to Muslims, rather, there was further increase in their oppression, the Final Messenger of Allah صَلَّى اللّٰہُ عَلَیْہِ وَاٰلِہٖ وَسَلَّم permitted his devoted companions to migrate to Abyssinia[3].[4]

Najashi, the king of Abyssinia, was the follower of the Christian faith, and was a just and a soft-hearted person. Therefore, in the fifth year of the declaration of Prophethood, a caravan consisting of eleven men and four women migrated to Abyssinia, leaving their beloved motherland.

1 Sharh al-Zurqaani 'alal-Mawahib, vol. 1, p. 498
2 Sharh al-Zurqaani 'alal-Mawahib, vol. 1, p. 496
3 Some areas of the current Ethiopia, situated in the African continent, were referred to as Abyssinia by the people of Arab. The king of Abyssinia, Najashi, who later was privileged to embrace Islam, was in rule there. His shrine is located in Ethiopia.
4 Sharh Zurqaani Alal-Mawahib, vol. 1, p. 502

It is called the First Migration. After a few days, many more male and female companions migrated to Abyssinia, to the extent that the number of those who migrated to Abyssinia rose to 82.[1]

Having seen this, the Quraysh sent a delegation to the king of Abyssinia, which insisted for the king to hand over the Muslims to Quraysh, but these efforts of the disbelievers were unsuccessful.[2]

Map of the route of migration to Abyssinia

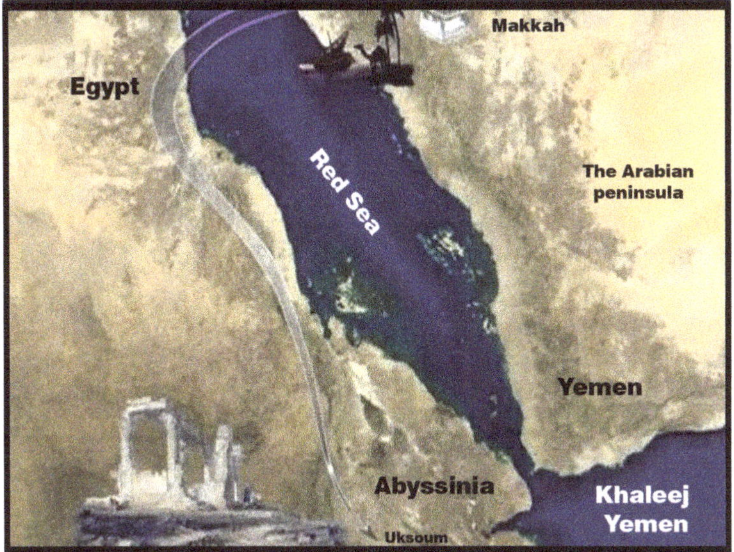

Masjid al-Najashi in Abyssinia

1 Sharh Zurqaani 'alal-Mawahib, vol. 2, p. 31

2 Sharh Zurqaani 'alal-Mawahib, vol. 1, p. 506

Chapter 7

Boycott and The year of grief

Siege of Shi'b Abi Taalib

The disbelievers of Makkah were under the illusion that they would either terminate or weaken the movement of Islam by their savage brutality and oppression, but despite all their efforts, the number of Muslims continued to rise. Due to this situation, Quraysh became absolutely infuriated.

All the chiefs of Quraysh and the other disbelievers of Makkah made a plan that they would completely boycott the Final Messenger of Allah صَلَّى اللّٰهُ عَلَيْهِ وَاٰلِهٖ وَسَلَّم and his family. Therefore, according to this plan, all the tribes of Quraysh made the following agreement: "No one will marry into the family of Banu Hashim, no one will do any kind of trade with them, and no one will socialise or converse with them or greet them or meet them, until the family of Banu Hashim hands the Beloved Prophet صَلَّى اللّٰهُ عَلَيْهِ وَاٰلِهٖ وَسَلَّم over to us. No one should let any food provisions reach them."

Mansoor Bin 'Ikramah wrote the agreement, all the chiefs of Quraysh signed it and hung it inside the *Ka'bah*.

Except Abu Lahab, all the people of Banu Hashim were besieged in the ravine of Abu Taalib, which is now called the Sh'ib of Abi Taalib. Non-Muslims were also among them who were with the Beloved Prophet صَلَّى اللّٰهُ عَلَيْهِ وَاٰلِهٖ وَسَلَّم only because of their family relation.[1]

All the people of Banu Hashim remained in that ravine for three years. These three years were so tough that Banu Hashim would eat leaves and cook dried skin to eat. Due to hunger, small children would cry so loudly that their voices could be heard at a far distance, but the stone-hearted disbelievers had placed guards over the ravine on all sides so that no food provision could reach inside the ravine.[2]

1 Sharh al-Zurqaani 'alal Mawahib, vol. 2, pp. 12 to 14
2 Seerat-e-Mustafa, p. 139

When three years passed by in the same state, Allah عَزَّوَجَلَّ gave His Beloved Prophet صَلَّى اللّٰهُ عَلَيْهِ وَاٰلِهٖ وَسَلَّم the news: "Termites have eaten and destroyed the agreement in a way that nothing has been left on it except for the name of Allah."

The Beloved Prophet صَلَّى اللّٰهُ عَلَيْهِ وَاٰلِهٖ وَسَلَّم gave this news to Abu Taalib and Abu Taalib went to the disbelievers of Quraysh, and said: "O the group of Quraysh! My nephew has given me the news in this way. Bring your agreement! If this news is true, then refrain from this oppression, and if this news is not true, then I will hand my nephew over to you."

They agreed to this. When they went there and saw it, they were absolutely amazed, because it was exactly the same, word to word, as the Beloved Prophet صَلَّى اللّٰهُ عَلَيْهِ وَاٰلِهٖ وَسَلَّم had stated.[1]

The Year of Grief

In the 10th year of the declaration of Prophethood, a short while after the end of the siege of the Sh'ib of Abi Taalib, Abu Taalib, the uncle of the Final Messenger of Allah صَلَّى اللّٰهُ عَلَيْهِ وَاٰلِهٖ وَسَلَّم, passed away. The Beloved Prophet صَلَّى اللّٰهُ عَلَيْهِ وَاٰلِهٖ وَسَلَّم was greatly grieved over the death of Abu Taalib.[2]

Not even a week had passed since the death of Abu Taalib, his wife, Sayyidatuna Khadija رَضِیَ اللّٰهُ عَنْهَا, also passed away. In Makkah, these two personages were the ones who were very close to him. They supported and helped him on every step.

When the Beloved Prophet صَلَّى اللّٰهُ عَلَيْهِ وَاٰلِهٖ وَسَلَّم kindled the flame of monotheism *[Tawheed]* in the darkness of disbelief and polytheism

1 Sharh Zurqaani 'alal-Mawahib, vol. 2, p. 37, summarised
2 Sharh Zurqaani 'alal-Mawahib, vol. 2, p. 38

[Kufr and Shirk], the disbelievers showed great insolence towards him; during these testing times, it was both these personages who became his support and shelter.

Their deaths occurred in the same year within a very short span of time, which deeply saddened and grieved the Prophet صَلَّى اللّٰهُ عَلَيْهِ وَاٰلِهٖ وَسَلَّم. He صَلَّى اللّٰهُ عَلَيْهِ وَاٰلِهٖ وَسَلَّم, therefore, called this year *'Aam-ul-Huzn'*, i.e. 'The Year of Grief'.

An old picture of Shi'b Abi Taalib. Now this place has been included in Masjid al-Haraam.

An old picture of the blessed shrine of Sayyidatuna Khadija al-Kubra رَضِیَ اللّٰهُ عَنْهَا

Chapter 8

Journey of Taif and Migration to Madinah

Events of the Journey of Taif

After the death of Sayyidatuna Khadija رَضِیَ اللّٰہُ عَنْہَا and Abu Taalib, the oppression and tyranny of the disbelievers increased even further. Due to this behaviour of theirs, the Beloved Prophet صَلَّی اللّٰہُ عَلَیْہِ وَاٰلِہٖ وَسَلَّم thought that if he goes to Taif and propagates Islam there, and if their chiefs embrace Islam, then it would give power and strength to the Muslims. Having thought this, he intended to travel to Ta`if.

He set out for Ta`if on foot. Only Sayyiduna Zaid Bin Harithah رَضِیَ اللّٰہُ عَنْہُ, his slave, was accompanying him. After reaching Ta`if, he صَلَّی اللّٰہُ عَلَیْہِ وَاٰلِہٖ وَسَلَّم rested for a few days and then met the chiefs of Ta`if.

He صَلَّی اللّٰہُ عَلَیْہِ وَاٰلِہٖ وَسَلَّم invited three chiefs—Abd Yaleel and his two brothers, Mas'ood and Habib—to Islam, but rejecting his invitation, not did they only ridicule him, but also made the wicked and mischievous people of Ta`if chase after him, who gathered in the form of a procession and started pursuing him.

They would make taunting remarks, utter immoral sentences, and chase after him raising the slogans of their idols, and they even started throwing stones at him.

They aimed at his blessed feet and threw so many stones at him that his blessed feet were wounded and started bleeding. His blessed feet bled so heavily that his blessed sandals were covered in blood. His slave, Sayyiduna Zaid Bin Harithah رَضِیَ اللّٰہُ عَنْہُ, put himself in front of him in order to guard him and take the stones upon his own body, due to which, he was also covered in blood.

When the Beloved Prophet صَلَّی اللّٰہُ عَلَیْہِ وَاٰلِہٖ وَسَلَّم would sit down due to the intensity of the pain, one of the mischievous people would move forward, and make him stand up by shaking him mercilessly, forcing him to walk. When he صَلَّى اللهُ عَلَيْهِ وَاٰلِهٖ وَسَلَّم would start walking, those cruel people would start stoning him again, abusing him, clapping and making fun of him.

Finally, he صَلَّى اللهُ عَلَيْهِ وَاٰلِهٖ وَسَلَّم took shelter with Zaid Bin Harithah رَضِیَ اللهُ عَنْهُ in a nearby grape orchard. It was the orchard of Utbah Bin Rabee'ah, a famous disbeliever and enemy. Seeing the condition of the Beloved Prophet صَلَّى اللهُ عَلَيْهِ وَاٰلِهٖ وَسَلَّم, even he looked at him with a merciful gaze. He sent a bunch of grapes through his slave, which the Beloved Prophet صَلَّى اللهُ عَلَيْهِ وَاٰلِهٖ وَسَلَّم accepted.

After listening to the Beloved Prophet صَلَّى اللهُ عَلَيْهِ وَاٰلِهٖ وَسَلَّم, the Christian slave 'Addaas, who brought the grapes, embraced faith upon him and started kissing his blessed hands and feet.[1]

This is Masjid 'Addaas, situated in Ta`if. It is said that it is the same place where the Beloved Prophet صَلَّى اللهُ عَلَيْهِ وَاٰلِهٖ وَسَلَّم took rest after being wounded. Remember, Ta`if is a city located at a distance of approximately 91 kilometres from Makkah. It is situated approx. 5,500 feet above the sea level. The weather is very pleasant here, and it is not as hot as the other areas of Arabia. The grapes and honey of Ta`if are very famous. It

1 Sharh al-Zurqaani alal-Mawahib, vol. 2, p. 49 to 56

is the first city of Arabia which was surrounded by walls.

Toughest day

After many years, once Sayyidatuna 'Aisha رَضِیَ اللہُ عَنْہَا asked the Final Messenger of Allah صَلَّى اللهُ عَلَيْهِ وَاٰلِهٖ وَسَلَّم: "Is there any other day for you that is tougher than even the day of the Battle of Uhud?" The Beloved Prophet صَلَّى اللهُ عَلَيْهِ وَاٰلِهٖ وَسَلَّم replied: "Yes, O 'Aisha! The day when I invited the chief "'Abd Ya'leel" to Islam in Ta`if was even tougher than the day of the Battle of Uhud for me. He did not accept the invitation of Islam and the people of Ta`if stoned me. I kept walking in this grief and sorrow with my head lowered, to the extent that I reached "Qarn al-Tha'alib", where I regained my breath. Having reached there, when I raised my head, what I saw was that a cloud has shaded me. Sayyiduna Jibraeel عَلَيْهِ السَّلَام called me from that cloud, and said: "Allah Almighty has heard the reply of your nation and now, the angel of mountains is present in your esteemed court so that he may carry out your command." Then, the angel of mountains gave *Salaam* to me and humbly said: "O Muhammad (صَلَّى اللهُ عَلَيْهِ وَاٰلِهٖ وَسَلَّم)! Allah Almighty has sent me to you so that whatever you command, I fulfil it. If you tell me to turn both, Mount Abu Qubays and Mount Qa'iqa'an, upside down onto these disbelievers, then I will do so." Having heard this, the Beloved Prophet صَلَّى اللهُ عَلَيْهِ وَاٰلِهٖ وَسَلَّم replied: "No, but rather, I am hopeful that Allah Almighty will create such people from their offspring who will only worship Allah Almighty and not commit polytheism."[1]

JINNS Embraced Islam

Upon returning from the journey of Ta`if, the Final Messenger of Allah صَلَّى اللهُ عَلَيْهِ وَاٰلِهٖ وَسَلَّم stayed at a place called "Nakhlah". When he صَلَّى اللهُ عَلَيْهِ وَاٰلِهٖ وَسَلَّم was reciting the Holy Quran during *Tahajjud Salah* at night, a group of *jinns* from Nasaybayn came to him and became

1 Sharh Zurqaani Alal-Mawahib, vol. 2, p. 51

Muslim after listening to the Holy Quran. Then those *jinns* returned to their nation and preached to them. So, many big groups of *jinns* in Makkah embraced Islam.[1]

In the Holy Quran, Allah Almighty has mentioned this account in the initial verses of *Surah Jinn*.

Light of Islam in Sacred Madinah

To the north of Makkah was a city, namely "Yathrib", which became "Madinah"[2] at a later stage. After the arrival of

1 Al-Mawahib-al-Ladunniyah, vol. 1, p. 137-138, summarised

2 The full name of Madinah is "Madina al-Nabi". The foundations of this city are based on Islam. Masjid al-Nabawi and the blessed shrine of the Prophet صَلَّى اللّٰهُ عَلَيۡهِ وَاٰلِهٖ وَسَلَّم are situated here. Now, the size of this city is almost 589 square kilometres. This city is located at a distance of almost 342 kilometres from Makkah, whereas nowadays, it is the travel of 450 kilometres by road. The Final Messenger of Allah صَلَّى اللّٰهُ عَلَيۡهِ وَاٰلِهٖ وَسَلَّم spent approx. 10 years of his apparent life here. This city is the coolness of the eyes of the devotees of the Prophet.

the Beloved Prophet صَلَّى اللّٰهُ عَلَيْهِ وَاٰلِهٖ وَسَلَّم there, its name became "Madinah". At the time of the declaration of Prophethood, there were two tribes there, "Aus" and "Khazraj", and some Jews were also living with them.

Though these people were idol worshippers, but they had learnt from the Jews that very soon, the Final Messenger of Allah صَلَّى اللّٰهُ تَعَالٰی عَلَيْهِ وَاٰلِهٖ وَسَلَّم would arrive. It was as if they were waiting for the arrival of the Beloved Prophet صَلَّى اللّٰهُ عَلَيْهِ وَاٰلِهٖ وَسَلَّم, so that they could adorn their fortune by believing in him.

In the 11th year of the declaration of Prophethood, the Beloved Prophet صَلَّى اللّٰهُ عَلَيْهِ وَاٰلِهٖ وَسَلَّم went to Mina in order to invite the tribes who were coming on the occasion of Hajj to Islam. There is a ravine in Mina where Masjid al-'Aqabah[1] is located today.

The Beloved Prophet صَلَّى اللّٰهُ عَلَيْهِ وَاٰلِهٖ وَسَلَّم was present there when six people from the tribe of Khazraj came to him. The Beloved Prophet صَلَّى اللّٰهُ عَلَيْهِ وَاٰلِهٖ وَسَلَّم asked them about their names and lineages. Then, he صَلَّى اللّٰهُ عَلَيْهِ وَاٰلِهٖ وَسَلَّم recited a few verses of the Holy Quran to them and then invited them to Islam, resulting in them being greatly impressed.

Upon their return, they said to each other: "Surely, he is the Final Messenger about whom the Jews keep talking. Therefore, let it not be the case that Jews embrace Islam before us." Having said this, they all became Muslim and went to Madinah, where they also invited their family members and relatives to Islam.

1 'Aqabah means ravine in Arabic.

Bay'at al 'Aqabah al-Oula[1]

In the next year, i.e. in the 12th year of the declaration of prophethood, on the occasion of Hajj, 12 more people from Madinah secretly embraced Islam in the ravine of Mina and pledged allegiance to the Beloved Prophet صَلَّى اللّٰہُ عَلَيۡهِ وَاٰلِهٖ وَسَلَّم. In the history of Islam, this *Bay'ah* [i.e. pledge] is called "*Bay'at al-'Aqabah al-Oula*" (i.e. the First *Bay'ah* of ravine).

This *Bay'ah* is called *Bay'at al-'Aqabah* because this *Bay'ah* was pledged on the mountain of Mina, near 'Aqabah, which is also called Jamra al-'Aqabah.[2]

They requested the Beloved Prophet صَلَّى اللّٰہُ عَلَيۡهِ وَاٰلِهٖ وَسَلَّم to provide them with a teacher who could teach them the commandments of Islam. The Beloved Prophet صَلَّى اللّٰہُ عَلَيۡهِ وَاٰلِهٖ وَسَلَّم sent Sayyiduna Mus'ab bin Umair رَضِیَ اللّٰہُ عَنۡهُ with them to Madinah. In Madina, he went to people's houses, inviting them to Islam, as a result of which, numerous people started embracing Islam on daily basis, to the extent that gradually, Islam started to spread everywhere.

Sayyiduna Sa'd Bin Mu'aaz رَضِیَ اللّٰہُ عَنۡهُ, the chief of the Aus tribe, also

1 The first pledge of 'Aqabah

2 Faizan-e-Siddeeq-e-Akbar, p. 199

embraced Islam through his invitation. As soon as he embraced Islam, his entire Aus tribe also became Muslim.[1]

Bay'at al-'Aqabah al-Thaniya[2]

After one year of this Bay'ah, i.e. in the 13th year of the declaration of Prophethood, on the occasion of Hajj, approximately 72 people of Madinah pledged allegiance to the Beloved Prophet صَلَّى اللّٰهُ عَلَيْهِ وَاٰلِهٖ وَسَلَّم secretly from their idol-worshipping friends, and promised that they would sacrifice their life and wealth, everything of theirs, for the protection of the Beloved Prophet صَلَّى اللّٰهُ عَلَيْهِ وَاٰلِهٖ وَسَلَّم and Islam.[3]

Migration to Madinah

With many people embracing Islam in Madinah, it was as though the Muslims had found a new shelter. The Beloved Prophet صَلَّى اللّٰهُ عَلَيْهِ وَاٰلِهٖ وَسَلَّم gave the blessed companions the total freedom to migrate to Madinah. Therefore, Sayyiduna Abu Salamah رَضِىَ اللّٰهُ عَنْهُ was the first one to migrate.[4] After him, other people also started migrating to Madinah.

When the disbelievers found out about this, they started their endeavours to prevent them from migrating, but people continued to migrate secretly, to the extent that within a short span of time, many companions migrated to Madinah. Now, only those were left in Makkah who were either imprisoned by the disbelievers or could not migrate to Madinah due to poverty.

Since the Final Messenger of Allah صَلَّى اللّٰهُ عَلَيْهِ وَاٰلِهٖ وَسَلَّم had not yet been commanded to migrate by Allah Almighty, hence, he صَلَّى اللّٰهُ عَلَيْهِ وَاٰلِهٖ وَسَلَّم

---

1 Al-Mawahibul al-Ladunniyah, vol. 1, p. 140-142, selected

2 The second pledge of 'Aqabah

3 *Al-Mawahib al-ladunniya, vol. 1, p. 143, selected*

4 Al-Mawahib al-ladunniyah, vol. 1, p. 143

also remained in Makkah. As per his command, Sayyiduna Abu Bakr Siddeeq رَضِیَ اللّٰہُ عَنْهُ and Sayyiduna Ali رَضِیَ اللّٰہُ عَنْهُ were also still staying in Makkah.

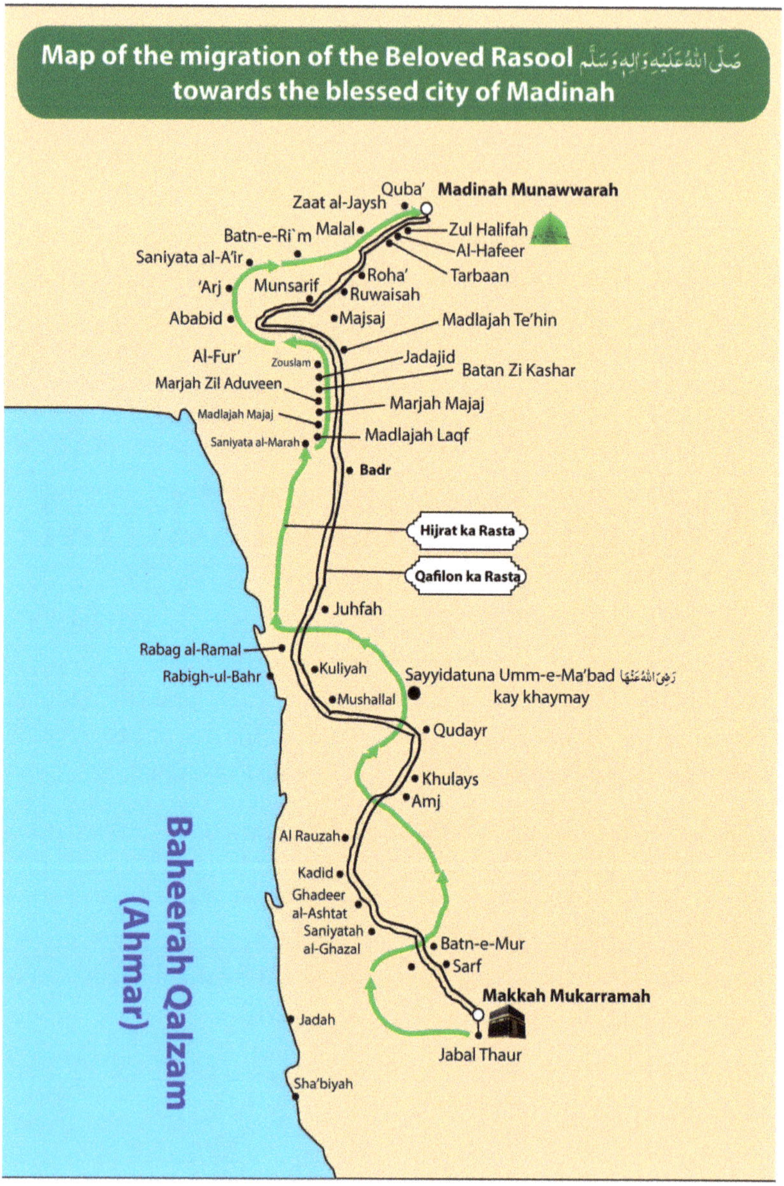

Map of the migration route of the Prophet صَلَّى اللّٰهُ عَلَيْهِ وَاٰلِهٖ وَسَلَّم to Madina

Council of Disbelievers

This entire situation left the disbelievers of Quraysh extremely worried. When they noticed that the people of Madinah had embraced Islam and were increasing in number, and the people of Makkah were also migrating there, they thought that if the Beloved Prophet صَلَّى اللّٰهُ عَلَيْهِ وَاٰلِهٖ وَسَلَّم also migrates there, then he might invade Makkah with an army of his supporters. Having felt this danger, the prominent chiefs of the Meccan disbelievers had a meeting in 'Dar al-Nadwah'.

All the elite intellectuals of the disbelievers attended that meeting. Different suggestions were given, out of which, the suggestion that Abu Jahl gave was accepted by everyone. His suggestion was that one young man from every tribe should be given a sword, and they all should attack the Beloved Prophet صَلَّى اللّٰهُ عَلَيْهِ وَاٰلِهٖ وَسَلَّم together and مَعَاذَاللّٰه martyr him. When the people from all the tribes would participate in it, then Banu Hashim would not be able to fight anyone, and they would agree upon receiving blood money.

There was a consensus upon this and the meeting came to an end. Sayyiduna Jibraeel عَلَيْهِ السَّلَام came with the command of Allah Almighty and informed the Prophet صَلَّى اللّٰهُ عَلَيْهِ وَاٰلِهٖ وَسَلَّم of this incident, and said: "Do not sleep in your bed tonight, and migrate to Madinah."

Migration *of the* Prophet صَلَّى اللّٰهُ عَلَيْهِ وَسَلَّم

At night, the disbelievers surrounded the blessed house of the Beloved Prophet صَلَّى اللّٰهُ عَلَيْهِ وَاٰلِهٖ وَسَلَّم according to their plan and started waiting for him to go to sleep so that they could attack him. At that time, only Sayyiduna Ali رَضِیَ اللّٰهُ عَنْهُ was present there.

Although the disbelievers were the enemies of the Beloved Prophet صَلَّى اللّٰهُ عَلَيْهِ وَاٰلِهٖ وَسَلَّم, but they had absolute trust in his trustworthiness and honesty. This was the reason why they would entrust their belongings to him. Even at that time, many entrusted belongings were kept at his blessed house.

The Final Messenger of Allah صَلَّى اللّٰهُ عَلَيْهِ وَاٰلِهٖ وَسَلَّم said to Sayyiduna Ali رَضِیَ اللّٰهُ عَنْهُ: "Sleep in my bed with my shawl over you! After I leave, hand all these entrustments to their owners, and then come to Madinah."

He صَلَّى اللّٰهُ عَلَيْهِ وَاٰلِهٖ وَسَلَّم took a fistful of soil, and reciting some initial verses of Surah Yaseen, he threw it at the disbelievers, and passed through the crowd of the disbelievers easily with no one even recognizing him.[1]

Then, he صَلَّى اللّٰهُ عَلَيْهِ وَاٰلِهٖ وَسَلَّم reached the Cave of Thaur with Sayyiduna Abu Bakr Siddeeq رَضِیَ اللّٰهُ عَنْهُ and stayed there for three days and three nights.[2] After this, he صَلَّى اللّٰهُ عَلَيْهِ وَاٰلِهٖ وَسَلَّم went to Madinah.

1 Al-Mawahib al-Ladunniyyah, vol. 1, p. 144, summarised
2 Bukhari, vol. 2, p. 593, Hadith 3905

Chapter 9

From Migration *to the* Treaty of Hudaybiyah

Beloved Prophet ﷺ in Madinah

The people of Madinah had received the news of the arrival of the Final Messenger of Allah صَلَّى اللهُ عَلَيْهِ وَاٰلِهٖ وَسَلَّم. They were desperately waiting for him, such that even the women and children of Madinah would talk about his arrival.

In those days, the distance between Makkah and Madinah would usually be covered in 12 days. They spent these days waiting, but after this, they could not help it anymore. Being restless and to fulfil their desire, they would gather in a field outside Madinah in order to welcome their master. When the sun would begin to blaze down, they would return to their homes wistfully. They followed this routine every day; they would come with a new determination and belief every day and stand in the pathways to welcome the Beloved Prophet صَلَّى اللهُ عَلَيْهِ وَاٰلِهٖ وَسَلَّم.

One day, as per routine, the people of Madinah had gone back after waiting for the Beloved Prophet صَلَّى اللهُ عَلَيْهِ وَاٰلِهٖ وَسَلَّم. Suddenly, a Jew saw from his fort that a caravan of people was approaching. When he saw the caravan, he understood, and then called out loudly: "O the people of Madinah! The merciful caravan that you have been waiting for every day has arrived." Having heard this, all the people of the Ansar, with their weapons on their bodies, came out of their homes happily in order to welcome the Final Messenger of Allah صَلَّى اللهُ عَلَيْهِ وَاٰلِهٖ وَسَلَّم.

Three miles away from Madina where "Masjid-e-Quba" is situated today, the Beloved Prophet صَلَّى اللهُ عَلَيْهِ وَاٰلِهٖ وَسَلَّم arrived there on 12th of *Rabi' al-Awwal*, and the 'Amr Bin 'Auf tribe was the fortunate tribe that the Prophet صَلَّى اللهُ عَلَيْهِ وَاٰلِهٖ وَسَلَّم first granted the privilege to host him.

The Beloved Prophet صَلَّى اللهُ عَلَيْهِ وَاٰلِهٖ وَسَلَّم stayed at the house of Sayyiduna Kulthoom Bin Hidm رَضِیَ اللهُ عَنْهُ, one of the chiefs of this tribe. Many companions who migrated to Madinah before were also staying in this house. After a few days of returning the entrustments of Quraysh, Sayyiduna Ali رَضِیَ اللّٰہُ عَنْہُ also left Makkah, and he also stayed in the same house.[1]

Construction of Masjid Quba *and the Start of* Jumu'ah Salah

The first thing that the Final Messenger of Allah صَلَّى اللهُ عَلَيْهِ وَاٰلِهٖ وَسَلَّم did in Quba was that he built a Masjid there. Sayyiduna Kulthoom Bin Hidm رَضِیَ اللّٰہُ عَنْہُ had an empty piece of land, which was used to dry dates. He صَلَّى اللهُ عَلَيْهِ وَاٰلِهٖ وَسَلَّم acquired that land and laid the foundation of a Masjid there. This Masjid is still known as "Masjid Quba" today.[2]

After staying there for more than two weeks, the Beloved Prophet صَلَّى اللهُ عَلَيْهِ وَاٰلِهٖ وَسَلَّم set out for Madinah. On the way, he صَلَّى اللهُ عَلَيْهِ وَاٰلِهٖ وَسَلَّم offered the first Jumu'ah Salah in the Masjid of the tribe Bani Salim. He then went to Madinah.

The Beloved Prophet صَلَّى اللهُ عَلَيْهِ وَاٰلِهٖ وَسَلَّم has stated: "To offer Salah in Quba Masjid is equal to an Umrah." *(Tirmizi, vol. 1, p. 348, Hadith 324)*

1 Dalaa`il-un-Nubuwwah by Bayhaqi, vol. 2, p. 499-500
2 Wafa-ul-Wafa, vol. 1, p. 250, selected

Stay in Madinah

When the Final Messenger of Allah صَلَّى اللّٰهُ عَلَيْهِ وَاٰلِهٖ وَسَلَّم arrived in Madinah, many Ansari companions requested him to stay at their homes, but he said: "Wherever Allah عَزَّوَجَلَّ wants, my (she-)camel will sit there."

His camel sat where Masjid al-Nabawi is situated today. The house of Sayyiduna Ayyub Ansari رَضِیَ اللّٰهُ عَنْهُ was situated nearby. Sayyiduna Abu Ayyub Ansari رَضِیَ اللّٰهُ عَنْهُ took the belongings of the Beloved Prophet صَلَّى اللّٰهُ عَلَيْهِ وَاٰلِهٖ وَسَلَّم to his home with his permission, and the Beloved Prophet صَلَّى اللّٰهُ عَلَيْهِ وَاٰلِهٖ وَسَلَّم stayed at his home.

Sayyiduna Abu Ayyub Ansari رَضِیَ اللّٰهُ عَنْهُ had the privilege of serving the Beloved Prophet صَلَّى اللّٰهُ عَلَيْهِ وَاٰلِهٖ وَسَلَّم for seven months. When Masjid al-Nabawi and its surrounding rooms were ready, then he صَلَّى اللّٰهُ عَلَيْهِ وَاٰلِهٖ وَسَلَّم began to reside there with his blessed wives.

Construction of Masjid al-Nabawi

There was no such place in Madinah where Muslims could offer *Salah* with *Jama'ah* [i.e. congregation]; therefore, it was very important to build a *masjid* there.

There was an orchard of "Banu Najjaar" near the blessed residence of the Final Messenger of Allah صَلَّى اللّٰهُ عَلَيْهِ وَاٰلِهٖ وَسَلَّم. That land was, in fact, owned by two orphan children. He صَلَّى اللّٰهُ عَلَيْهِ وَاٰلِهٖ وَسَلَّم called both the orphan children. They both wanted to donate the land for the *masjid*, but the Final Messenger of Allah صَلَّى اللّٰهُ عَلَيْهِ وَاٰلِهٖ وَسَلَّم did not approve it, and paid its price from the wealth of Sayyiduna Abu Bakr Siddeeq رَضِیَ اللّٰهُ عَنْهُ.

Levelling the ground, the Beloved Prophet صَلَّى اللّٰهُ عَلَيْهِ وَاٰلِهٖ وَسَلَّم laid the foundation of the *masjid* with his own blessed hands, had a wall made of unbaked bricks, and a roof with date leaves built on the pillars of date trees. The roof would leak during the rain. For the construction of this *masjid*, the Holy Prophet صَلَّى اللهُ عَلَيْهِ وَاٰلِهٖ وَسَلَّم would also bring bricks along with the blessed companions.[1]

Adhan was also initiated from here. In the beginning, Sayyiduna Bilal رَضِیَ اللهُ عَنْهُ would call Muslims for Salah. Then, Sayyiduna Abdullah bin Zaid Ansari رَضِیَ اللهُ عَنْهُ and other companions رَضِیَ اللهُ عَنْهُم heard the words of *Adhan* in their dream. With the command of the Beloved Prophet صَلَّى اللهُ عَلَيْهِ وَاٰلِهٖ وَسَلَّم, Sayyiduna Abdullah bin Zaid رَضِیَ اللهُ عَنْهُ taught Sayyiduna Bilal رَضِیَ اللهُ عَنْهُ those words, and he started calling out the *Adhan*.[2]

The method of *Shar'i Adhan* was initiated on that very day, which is still being followed, and will continue to be followed until the Day of Judgement.

1 Bukhari, vol. 1, p. 165, Hadith 428 | Mawahib-ul-Ladunniya, vol. 1, p. 156 to 161, selected and summarised

2 Al-Mawahib al-Ladunniyyah, vol. 2, p. 163

Ansar and *Muhajir*,
Brothers of Each Other

Up till now, the total number of *Muhajireen* in Madinah was 45 or 50. Their state was such that they were destitute, and their families and wealth were all left in Makkah.

The Ansar although were very hospitable to them, but the *Muhajireen* did not like to live their life by relying upon others for a long time. Therefore, the Final Messenger of Allah صَلَّى اللهُ عَلَيْهِ وَاٰلِهٖ وَسَلَّم resolved this matter by establishing brotherhood between *Muhajireen* and *Ansar*, making them brothers of each other, so that they become helpers of each other.

Therefore, after the construction of Masjid al-Nabawi, one day, the Beloved Prophet صَلَّى اللهُ عَلَيْهِ وَاٰلِهٖ وَسَلَّم gathered the *Ansar* and *Muhajireen* companions at the home of Sayyiduna Anas Bin Malik رَضِیَ اللهُ عَنْهُ. Addressing the *Ansaar*, he صَلَّى اللهُ عَلَيْهِ وَاٰلِهٖ وَسَلَّم said: "The *Muhajireen* are your brothers." Then, he صَلَّى اللهُ عَلَيْهِ وَاٰلِهٖ وَسَلَّم kept calling one person each from the *Ansar* and *Muhajireen*, and saying: "You both are brothers." As soon as the Beloved Prophet صَلَّى اللهُ عَلَيْهِ وَاٰلِهٖ وَسَلَّم established this brotherhood, it became absolutely like the relationship between actual brothers. Therefore, the *Ansar* took their *Muhajir* brothers to their homes and placed one set of everything of their home before them, and said: "As you are our brothers, half of the things of our homes are yours and half are ours."[1]

Change of *Qiblah*

As long as the Final Messenger of Allah صَلَّى اللهُ عَلَيْهِ وَاٰلِهٖ وَسَلَّم remained in Makkah, he continued to offer *Salah* facing the Holy *Ka'bah*. After the migration, in Madinah, he would face "*Bayt al-Muqaddas*" in every *Salah* as per the Divine commandment.

1 Bukhari, vol. 2, p. 555, Hadith 3781

In the same state, 16 or 17 months passed by. He صَلَّى اللّٰهُ عَلَيْهِ وَاٰلِهٖ وَسَلَّم had this desire that the Holy *Ka'bah* be made the *Qiblah*. Therefore, one day, when the Final Messenger of Allah صَلَّى اللّٰهُ عَلَيْهِ وَاٰلِهٖ وَسَلَّم was leading the *Zuhr Salah* in the *Masjid* of the Bani Salama tribe, the following revelation was revealed upon him during the *Salah*:

قَدْ نَرٰى تَقَلُّبَ وَجْهِكَ فِی السَّمَآءِ ۚ فَلَنُوَلِّیَنَّكَ قِبْلَةً تَرْضٰىهَا ۪ فَوَلِّ وَجْهَكَ شَطْرَ الْمَسْجِدِ الْحَرَامِ

We are observing the turning of your face repeatedly towards the sky, so We will definitely turn you towards that Qiblah in which you are (more) pleased. Now, turn your face towards Masjid Haraam/Sacred Masjid (i.e. the Ka'bah).[1]

The Final Messenger of Allah صَلَّى اللّٰهُ عَلَيْهِ وَاٰلِهٖ وَسَلَّم turned his face from *Bayt al-Muqaddas* to the Holy *Ka'bah* during the Salah, and all the *Muqtadees*[2] also followed him. The Masjid in which this event took place is called 'Masjid al-Qiblatayn'. Even today, this Masjid and both of its prayer niches exist.

This Masjid is located approximately 2 kilometres away from Madinah towards the Northwest. The same event is called "*Tahweel al-Qiblah*". The Jews and hypocrites were greatly troubled due to *Tahweel al-Qiblah*.[3]

---

1 *[Kanz-ul-Iman (translation of Quran)] (Part 2, Surah Al-Baqarah, Verse 144)*

2 Those offering *salah* behind the Imam.

3 Madarij-un-Nubuwwat, part 3, chapter 2, vol. 2, p. 73, summarised

Conspiracies of Disbelievers and Steps Taken by Muslims

After Muslims' migration to Madinah, the disbelievers of Makkah should have now been at ease, but their fury increased even further. Now, they became enemies of the people of Madinah as well.

They wrote a letter to Abdullah bin Ubayy, the chief of the *Ansar*, saying: "Either expel the Muslims from Madinah or kill them, otherwise, we will attack you and make you face our swords."[1]

In the same way, when the chief of the Aws tribe went to Makkah to perform *'Umrah*, he was also threatened by the disbelievers of Makkah. The disbelievers did not only suffice upon threats, but they actually started preparing to attack Madinah. They conveyed this message to all the tribes that they would attack Madinah and kill all the Muslims. Under these circumstances, it became necessary for Muslims to do something for their own protection.

Up till now, the Final Messenger of Allah صَلَّى اللّٰهُ عَلَيْهِ وَاٰلِهٖ وَسَلَّم kept inviting people to Islam only through proofs and advice, as per the Divine commandment, and observed patience upon the calamities afflicted by the disbelievers. However, after the migration, when the entire Arabian Peninsula and all the Jews became the enemies of the Muslims and started devising different conspiracies to eradicate them, Allah Almighty gave the Muslims permission to fight war against those who start it.

Under these circumstances, the Beloved Prophet صَلَّى اللّٰهُ عَلَيْهِ وَاٰلِهٖ وَسَلَّم focused on two things:

1. The trade caravans of the people of Makkah which used to go to the Levant should be stopped and this route should be

1 Sunan Abi Dawood, vol. 3, p. 212, Hadith 3004

blocked, so that they could agree upon reconciliation.

2. A reconciliation treaty should be made with the surrounding tribes so that the disbelievers would not even dare to attack Madinah.

For this reason, the Beloved Prophet صَلَّى اللّٰهُ عَلَيْهِ وَاٰلِهٖ وَسَلَّم would also go himself to the surrounding tribes and also send small groups of troops who would keep an eye on the movement of the disbelievers of Makkah, and also make peace treaties with the tribes.

Due to this, Muslims started having clashes with the disbelievers of Makkah and their allies, and small and large battles began. These very battles are called "Ghazawat and Sarayah" in the history of Islam.

Difference Between Ghazwah and Sariyyah

The battle in which the Final Messenger of Allah صَلَّى اللّٰهُ عَلَيْهِ وَاٰلِهٖ وَسَلَّم personally participated is called a "*Ghazwah*", whereas, the battle in which the Beloved Prophet صَلَّى اللّٰهُ عَلَيْهِ وَاٰلِهٖ وَسَلَّم did not participate is called a "*Sariyyah*". The plural of *Ghazwah* is "*Ghazawaat*", and the plural of *Sariyyah* is "*Saraya*".[1]

There is a difference of opinion regarding the total number of *Ghazawaat* and *Saraya*. According to the narration of Imam Bukhari, there are 19 *Ghazawat*, out of which only 9 reached the stage of battle, whereas, the majority were such that did not require any actual combat.[2] The total number of *Saraya* is either 47 or 56.[3]

1 Madarij-un-Nubuwwat, part 3, chapter 2, vol. 2, p. 76
2 Bukhari, vol. 3, p. 3, Hadith 3949
3 Sharh Al-Zurqaani 'Ala-Al-Mawahib, vol. 2, p. 221

Causes of the Battle of

BADR

The first major battle which took place between the Muslims and the disbelievers is called "the *Ghazwa* of Badr".

Badr[1] is the name of a village that is situated at some distance from Madinah. There was a well there, and the name of the owner of that well was Badr. For this reason, this place became famous as Badr.[2]

Even before the Battle of Badr, some small and large skirmishes did take place between the Muslims and disbelievers. Once, a small group of disbelievers came to the pastures of Madinah and carried out plundering, whereas in one fight, a disbeliever was also killed. This death made the disbelievers of Makkah uncontrollably furious. The Battle of Badr took place due to their reaction.

Another cause for the Battle of Badr was that the news reached Madinah of a big caravan of disbelievers returning imminently to Makkah from the Levent. Many prominent chiefs of the disbelievers were in the caravan and they also had a lot of trade goods. The Final Messenger of Allah صَلَّى اللّٰهُ عَلَيْهِ وَاٰلِهٖ وَسَلَّم said: "Small groups of disbelievers remain in our pursuit, and one of their small groups even committed plundering in Madinah. Therefore, why not attack this caravan of Quraysh. This way, their trade route to the Levant will be blocked and they will be forced to make peace with us." Listening to his suggestion, all the *Muhajireen* and *Ansaar* became prepared for it.

Therefore, on 12th of Ramadan, 2 Hijri, the Beloved Prophet صَلَّى اللّٰهُ عَلَيْهِ وَاٰلِهٖ وَسَلَّم set out without any big preparation for the battle. Everyone set out in whatever state they were. This army of Muslims neither had many weapons nor any large amount of military ration,

1 Badr is 113 kilometres away from Madinah, and this distance is approximately 152 kilometres by road.

2 Sharh Al-Zurqaani 'Ala-Al-Mawahib, vol. 2, p. 255

because no one had assumed that there would be a major battle during this journey.

When the people of Makkah heard the news that the Muslims had left Madinah, they also started preparing for the battle. When the Beloved Prophet صَلَّى اللّٰهُ عَلَيْهِ وَاٰلِهٖ وَسَلَّم received this news, he consulted with the blessed companions, telling them that there is a possibility of a battle breaking out during this journey. The *Muhajireen* and the *Ansar* both expressed their determination that they would obey and protect the Beloved Prophet صَلَّى اللّٰهُ عَلَيْهِ وَاٰلِهٖ وَسَلَّم.

He صَلَّى اللّٰهُ عَلَيْهِ وَاٰلِهٖ وَسَلَّم reviewed the troops one mile away from Madinah, and ordered young children to go back. After taking some necessary measures, he صَلَّى اللّٰهُ عَلَيْهِ وَاٰلِهٖ وَسَلَّم headed towards the field of Badr, where the disbelievers of Makkah were to come from.

Now, the total number of the army was 313— 60 of which were *Muhajirin* and the rest were *Ansaar*. Abu Sufyan, on the other hand, also received the news that the Muslims had left. When he heard the news, he did two things. (1). He sent a person immediately to Makkah to inform Quraysh about this, so that they could make arrangements for the safety of their caravan. (2). He himself changed his route and set out with the caravan towards the sea.[1] As

1 Sharh Al-Zurqaani 'Ala-Al-Mawahib, vol. 2, p. 263

soon as Quraysh received the message of Abu Sufyan, they came out of their homes.

Map of the battle of Badr

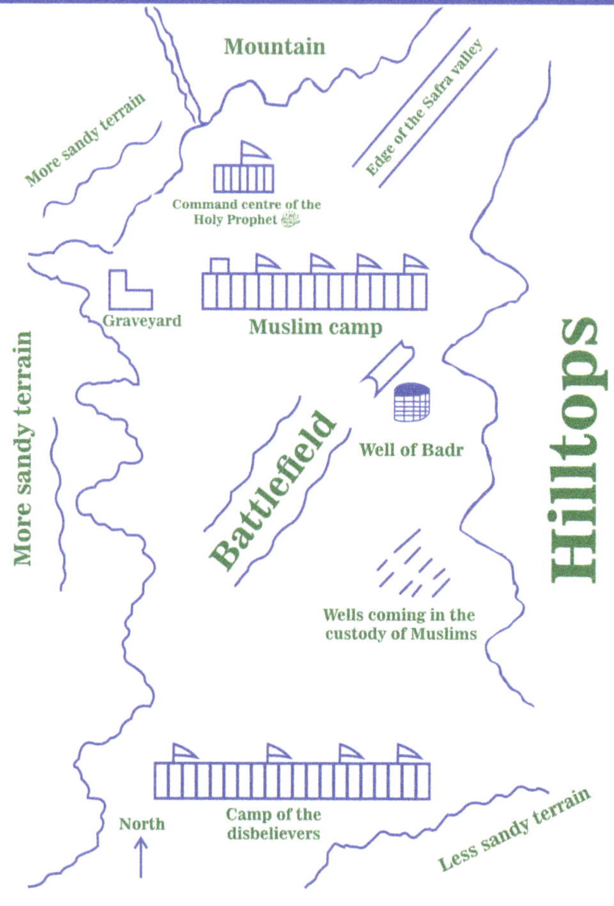

The chiefs of Quraysh set out with an army of one thousand armed troops. They arranged rations for the troops in a way that the rich people of Quraysh would slaughter ten camels every day and feed the troops.

Utbah Bin Rabi'ah, who was the richest person in Quraysh, was the commander in chief of this army. On the way, Abu Sufyan sent a message that we have made our caravan safe, therefore, the remaining people should return. He also added that there is no need to fight now. Some people of Quraysh agreed to return, but some of them insisted on fighting, and convinced some of the tribes too.

The disbelievers of Quraysh reached the plain of Badr before the Muslims and occupied the better and suitable places for themselves, whereas, the Muslims could not get a suitable place from the perspective of a battle.

Glory be to Allah! In the meantime, it rained, causing the dust and sand of the field to become hard, due to which, it became easier for the Muslims to walk on it, and the ground of the disbelievers became muddy, due to which, they faced great difficulty in walking and manoeuvring.

Who Will Die, and Where Will He Die, in the Battle of Badr?

The Final Messenger of Allah صَلَّى اللهُ عَلَيْهِ وَاٰلِهٖ وَسَلَّم came to inspect the battlefield in the night with some of his ardent devotees. He drew lines with a stick on the ground and said: "So-and-so disbeliever will be killed here; the dead

body of so-and-so will be here."

Therefore, exactly the same happened. The dead body of every disbeliever was found at the place where the Beloved Prophet صَلَّى اللّٰهُ عَلَيْهِ وَاٰلِهٖ وَسَلَّم had already stated.

The Battle of Badr and its Outcome

On Friday 17th Ramadan, 2 Hijri, corresponding to 13th March, 624 C.E, the Beloved Prophet صَلَّى اللّٰهُ عَلَيْهِ وَاٰلِهٖ وَسَلَّم ordered the Islamic warriors to be arrayed. The battle began, and despite having no provisions, the blessed companions رَضِیَ اللّٰهُ عَنْهُم showed great bravery and valour. In this battle, Abu Jahl was killed by two young companions, Sayyiduna Mu'aaz and Sayyiduna Mu'awwaz رَضِیَ اللّٰهُ عَنْهُمَا.

Many prominent chiefs of disbelievers, such as Abu Jahl, Utbah, Shaybah, etc., were killed in the battlefield, due to which, they lost their strength. They lost their courage, control, and fled after surrendering.

The Muslims started arresting the disbelievers. In this battle, seventy disbelievers were killed and the same number of disbelievers were held captives. The caravan of Abu Sufyan fled, but Muslims achieved a great success in this battle, which increased their grandeur and dignity.

All the respect and honour of the disbelievers was tarnished due to the defeat in this battle. Their military power was destroyed and their prominent chiefs were killed. After the conquest, the Beloved Prophet صَلَّى اللّٰهُ عَلَيْهِ وَاٰلِهٖ وَسَلَّم stayed in Badr for three days, and then set out for Madinah with the captives and the spoils of war.

Martyrs of Badr

In the Battle of Badr, fourteen Muslims were martyred - six *Muhajirin* and eight *Ansar*. Thirteen companions رَضِیَ اللّٰہُ عَنۡہُم were buried in the field of Badr, whereas, one companion, Sayyiduna Ubaydah Bin Harith رَضِیَ اللّٰہُ عَنۡہُ, passed away on the way, and his blessed shrine is located in "Safra"[1]. At the same place, the Beloved Prophet صَلَّى اللّٰهُ عَلَيْهِ وَاٰلِهٖ وَسَلَّم distributed the spoils of war amongst the *Mujahideen*.

The companions رَضِیَ اللّٰہُ عَنۡہُم who participated in the Battle of Badr have a special status and rank, and they all have great virtues. One of the virtues is that the Final Messenger of Allah صَلَّى اللّٰهُ عَلَيْهِ وَاٰلِهٖ وَسَلَّم said: "Undoubtedly, Allah Almighty is aware of the people of Badr, and He has said that, 'You may do whatever you like now. Indeed, Paradise has become *Wajib* for you,' or (He said) that, 'I have forgiven you'."[2]

Consequence *of the* Captives

The Final Messenger of Allah صَلَّى اللّٰهُ عَلَيْهِ وَاٰلِهٖ وَسَلَّم distributed the captives of Badr amongst the blessed companions so that the captives could take care of their comfort and needs. After consulting about the prisoners,

1 Sharh al-Zurqaani 'Ala-Al-Mawahib, vol. 2, pp. 325 - 328, summarised and selected

2 Bukhari, vol. 3, p. 12, Hadith 3983

it was decided that they would be released after taking 4,000 dirhams from each of them as *Fidya* (amount paid for the release of a prisoner).

Those who could not pay the *Fidya* amount because of poverty were released without the *Fidya*. As for those captives who knew how to write, their *Fidya* was that they should teach 10 boys of Ansar how to write.

Causes of the **Battle of Uhud** and the **Number of Soldiers**

Straight after returning from the Battle of Badr, the disbelievers started preparing for the next battle in order to take revenge. They prepared for the next battle for a whole year. In the 3rd year of the migration of the Prophet, in the month of *Shawwal*, the disbelievers of Quraysh prepared fully and set out with a big and strong army in every way with the intention to fight a war. Abu Sufyan (who had not yet embraced Islam) became the commander-in-chief of that army. Sayyiduna Abbas رَضِیَ اللہُ عَنْہُ, the uncle of the Beloved Prophet صَلَّی اللہُ عَلَیْہِ وَاٰلِہٖ وَسَلَّم who had secretly embraced Islam and lived in Makkah, wrote a letter and informed the Muslims about the army of the disbelievers.[1]

When the Beloved Prophet صَلَّی اللہُ عَلَیْہِ وَاٰلِہٖ وَسَلَّم investigated this, he found out that the army of disbelievers had arrived very close to Madinah. In this situation, he صَلَّی اللہُ عَلَیْہِ وَاٰلِہٖ وَسَلَّم consulted with the blessed companions رَضِیَ اللہُ عَنْہُم.

The senior companions gave the suggestion that they should fight against the enemies in the city, but the youth wanted to fight in the open. Having heard this suggestion, the Beloved Prophet صَلَّی اللہُ عَلَیْہِ وَاٰلِہٖ وَسَلَّم put his weapons on and came out. In the meanwhile, all the people had agreed to fight the disbelievers staying inside the city, but the Holy Prophet صَلَّی اللہُ عَلَیْہِ وَاٰلِہٖ وَسَلَّم said: "It is not befitting for a Prophet of Allah to remove weapons

1 Kitab al-Maghazi by Waqidi, vol. 1, p. 203

after wearing them, until Allah Almighty makes a decision between him and his enemies. Therefore, now with the name of Allah, leave for the (battle)field.”

The Beloved Prophet صَلَّى اللّٰهُ عَلَيْهِ وَاٰلِهٖ وَسَلَّم left Madinah with an army of one thousand soldiers. On the way, the hypocrite Abdullah Bin Ubayy, separated from the Islamic army along with his 300 soldiers. Now, the number in the Muslim army dropped to 700.

The Beloved Prophet صَلَّى اللّٰهُ عَلَيْهِ وَاٰلِهٖ وَسَلَّم examined the army and ordered the underaged companions to return.[1]

Map of the Battle of Uhud	Mount Uhud

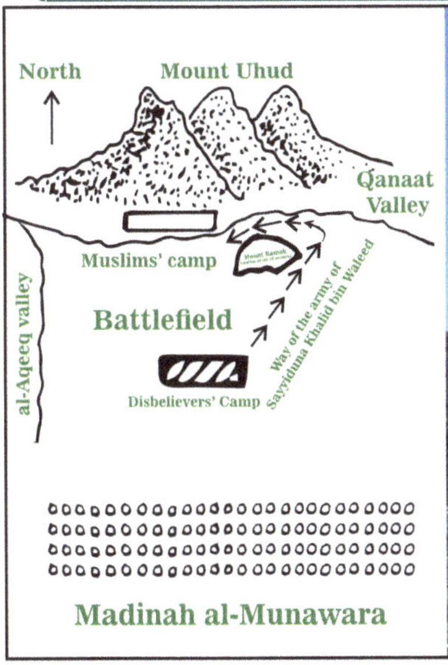

Mount Uhud is a range of mountains in the north of Madinah al-Munawwarah, extending from around six to seven kilometres. Its width is 2 to 3 kilometres and height is 350 meters. It is approximately 5 kilometres away from Masjid al-Nabawi. According to a Hadith, it is a heavenly mountain which loves the Beloved Prophet صَلَّى اللّٰهُ عَلَيْهِ وَاٰلِهٖ وَسَلَّم, and the Beloved Prophet صَلَّى اللّٰهُ عَلَيْهِ وَاٰلِهٖ وَسَلَّم loves it too. The Battle of Uhud (according to one narration) took place at the foot of this mountain on 17th Shawwal, 3 Hijri, corresponding to 23rd March, 625 C.E.

1 Sharh Al-Zurqaani ʻAla-Al-Mawahib, vol. 2, pp. 394 to 419, selected and summarised

Armies, FACE *to* FACE

The polytheists had already camped on Mount Uhud, near Madinah, on the 12th of Shawwal. The Final Messenger of Allah صَلَّى اللّٰهُ عَلَيْهِ وَاٰلِهٖ وَسَلَّم set out from Madinah on Friday 14th Shawwal, and reached Uhud on Saturday 15th Shawwal, at the time of Fajr.

After *Fajr Salah*, he صَلَّى اللّٰهُ عَلَيْهِ وَاٰلِهٖ وَسَلَّم arranged the army. At the time of arranging them, he صَلَّى اللّٰهُ عَلَيْهِ وَاٰلِهٖ وَسَلَّم kept Mount Uhud behind him.

Behind the army in the mountain was a narrow passage, through which the disbelievers of Quraysh could have attacked the Muslim troops. For this reason, the Holy Prophet صَلَّى اللّٰهُ عَلَيْهِ وَاٰلِهٖ وَسَلَّم deployed a group of 50 archers there for the protection of this passage. Sayyiduna Abdullah Bin Jubayr رَضِیَ اللّٰهُ عَنْهُ was given the command of this battalion and was ordered: "Whether we win or lose, do not leave this place."

Start of the Battle

When the battle began, the Muslims displayed such skills and expertise of bravery and valour that the disbelievers fled, facing defeat; but in the meantime, due to only one mistake, the whole situation of the battle changed.

When the archers, who were deployed upon the task of protecting the narrow passage on the mountain, saw that the battle has been won, they too joined the other companions to gather the spoils of war. Their commander-in-chief stopped them, but they thought that the battle has now ended, so there is no need to stay there anymore.

When Sayyiduna Khalid Bin Waleed, who had not yet embraced

Islam, saw that narrow passage without any guard, he attacked the Muslims from behind (through that narrow passage).

Sayyiduna Abdullah Bin Jubayr رَضِیَ اللّٰہُ عَنْہُ, along with a few companions, fought very bravely, but they all were martyred. Having seen the changed circumstances of the war, the fleeing army of the disbelievers of Quraish returned. This sudden attack changed the entire situation.[1]

Some Incidents of the Battle of Uhud

During the battle, a disbeliever struck his sword on the luminous face of the Beloved Prophet صَلَّی اللّٰہُ عَلَیْہِ وَاٰلِہٖ وَسَلَّم, due to which, some pieces of the casque (i.e. helmet) pierced his blessed face. Due to being hit by a stone, some corners of his blessed teeth also broke, and his blessed lower lip was also injured.

The disbelievers tried their best to martyr the Final Messenger of Allah صَلَّی اللّٰہُ عَلَیْہِ وَاٰلِہٖ وَسَلَّم, but they could not achieve their evil purpose. The honourable companions protected the Beloved Prophet صَلَّی اللّٰہُ عَلَیْہِ وَاٰلِہٖ وَسَلَّم valiantly.

When the battle ended, the disbelievers left from there, whereas the Muslims started to search for their martyrs. Seeing the martyrs severely distressed the Muslims. The number of martyrs in this *ghazwah* was seventy—Four of which were *Muhajirin* and sixty-six were *Ansar*. All these martyrs were buried at the foot of Mount Uhud. Two martyrs were buried in one grave. Thirty disbelievers were killed in this battle.[2]

1 Al-Iktifa, vol. 1, p. 377

2 Sharh al-Zurqaani 'Ala-Al-Mawahib, vol.2 p. 419, Madarij-un-Nubuwwah, vol. 2, p. 133

The Incident of Raji'

This heartrending incident occurred in the fourth year of migration. A few people from the tribe, 'Adal Waqarah, came to the Final Messenger of Allah صَلَّى اللّٰهُ عَلَيْهِ وَاٰلِهٖ وَسَلَّم, and humbly said: "Our tribe has embraced Islam. Please send some companions (رَضِیَ اللّٰهُ عَنْهُم) who can teach them about Islam."

The Beloved Prophet صَلَّى اللّٰهُ عَلَيْهِ وَاٰلِهٖ وَسَلَّم sent a group of ten companions رَضِیَ اللّٰهُ عَنْهُم with them. When this caravan reached the area of Raji'[1], the disbelievers deceivingly martyred eight of them, and sold the remaining two companions in Makkah.[2]

The Incident of Bir Ma'una

The famous incident of "Bir Ma'una" took place in the *Safar* of 4 *Hijri*. Amir bin Maalik, who was known for his bravery, came to the Final Messenger of Allah صَلَّى اللّٰهُ عَلَيْهِ وَاٰلِهٖ وَسَلَّم. The Holy Prophet صَلَّى اللّٰهُ عَلَيْهِ وَاٰلِهٖ وَسَلَّم invited him towards Islam, but he neither accepted it nor expressed hatred towards it, rather, he requested for some selected companions be sent with him.

The Beloved Prophet صَلَّى اللّٰهُ عَلَيْهِ وَاٰلِهٖ وَسَلَّم said: "I feel danger from the disbelievers of Najd." He said: "I assure you for the life and possessions of your companions." The Beloved Prophet صَلَّى اللّٰهُ عَلَيْهِ وَاٰلِهٖ وَسَلَّم sent seventy companions.

When these blessed companions reached Bir Ma'una, the leader of

1 There is a place between 'Usfaan and Makkah, called Raj'i. 'Usfaan is at a distance of 380 kilometres from Madinah and 93 kilometres from Makkah.

2 Madarij-un-Nubuwwah, part 3, chapter 4, vol. 2, p. 138, selected

the caravan went to 'Amir Bin Tufail, who was the nephew of 'Amir Bin Malik, with the letter of the Beloved Prophet صَلَّى اللّٰهُ عَلَيْهِ وَاٰلِهٖ وَسَلَّم. Amir Bin Tufail deceivingly had him martyred too, and attacked the rest of the companions رَضِیَ اللّٰهُ عَنْهُم with the help of the nearby tribes. They left only one companion, Sayyiduna 'Amr Bin Umayyah رَضِیَ اللّٰهُ عَنْهُ, and martyred the rest of the companions رَضِیَ اللّٰهُ عَنْهُم.

The Final Messenger of Allah صَلَّى اللّٰهُ عَلَيْهِ وَاٰلِهٖ وَسَلَّم was deeply grieved when he (Sayyiduna 'Amr bin Umayyah) reached Madinah and related the entire incident to him.

The Ghazwah of Banu Nadeer

Whilst returning from Bir Ma'una, Sayyiduna 'Amr Bin Umayyah رَضِیَ اللّٰهُ عَنْهُ killed two disbelievers who had been given refuge by the Final Messenger of Allah صَلَّى اللّٰهُ عَلَيْهِ وَاٰلِهٖ وَسَلَّم. He thought that he had taken back the revenge of the companions who were martyred in Bir Ma'una, but he later found out about the reality.

The Final Messenger of Allah صَلَّى اللّٰهُ عَلَيْهِ وَاٰلِهٖ وَسَلَّم announced that blood money of those two disbelievers would be paid. To discuss this matter, he صَلَّى اللّٰهُ عَلَيْهِ وَاٰلِهٖ وَسَلَّم went to the Jews of the tribe Banu Nadeer, because his agreement was with them.

Outwardly, they showed very kind behaviour, but plotted a trap in such a way that they made the Final Messenger of Allah صَلَّى اللّٰهُ عَلَيْهِ وَاٰلِهٖ وَسَلَّم and the blessed companions sit beside a wall with great respect and reverence, and sent a person upstairs to drop a heavy stone on them so that they all get martyred.

Allah عَزَّوَجَلَّ informed the Beloved Prophet صَلَّى اللّٰهُ عَلَيْهِ وَاٰلِهٖ وَسَلَّم of this plan. He صَلَّى اللّٰهُ عَلَيْهِ وَاٰلِهٖ وَسَلَّم stood up immediately without saying anything and returned with his companions. After reaching Madinah, he صَلَّى اللّٰهُ عَلَيْهِ وَاٰلِهٖ وَسَلَّم informed the blessed companions about this conspiracy of the Jews.

After consulting with the *Ansar* and *Muhajireen*, the Beloved Prophet صَلَّى اللّٰهُ عَلَيْهِ وَاٰلِهٖ وَسَلَّم sent a message to the Jews, saying that you have broken the agreement by plotting a conspiracy, therefore, leave Madinah within ten days.

The Jews refused to do so. When they refused to do so, the Beloved Prophet صَلَّى اللّٰهُ عَلَيْهِ وَاٰلِهٖ وَسَلَّم left with an army and besieged the fort of the Jews. This siege continued for fifteen days. During this siege, the Beloved Prophet صَلَّى اللّٰهُ عَلَيْهِ وَاٰلِهٖ وَسَلَّم got some trees around the fort cut, so that the Jews do not harm the Muslim army by hiding in the trees.

Being helpless, the Jews agreed to leave their houses and the fort, but said that they will take as many belongings of theirs as they can by loading them on their camels.

The Beloved Prophet صَلَّى اللّٰهُ عَلَيْهِ وَاٰلِهٖ وَسَلَّم accepted this condition of theirs, and all the Jews of Banu Nadeer, except for two people who embraced Islam, left Madinah in the form of a procession singing and playing music after loading their belongings and provisions onto six hundred camels. Some of them settled in Khayber, whereas, some went to the Levant and settled there.[1]

The Battle of Banu Mustaliq and the Incident of Ifk

At a great distance from Madinah, a branch of the tribe Khaza'ah, '*Banu Mustaliq*'[2], dwelled. In Sha'ban of 5 Hijri, when the chief of this tribe intended to invade Madinah, the Beloved Prophet صَلَّى اللّٰهُ عَلَيْهِ وَاٰلِهٖ وَسَلَّم went with his army to fight him. When they found out about the arrival of the Beloved Prophet صَلَّى اللّٰهُ عَلَيْهِ وَاٰلِهٖ وَسَلَّم, their

1 Sharh al-Zurqaani 'Ala-Al-Mawahib, vol. 2, p. 497-520, selected and summarised

2 Now, the distance of this place from Madinah is 261 kilometres.

chief fled out of fear. Other people of the tribe tried to fight, but when the Muslims attacked together, ten disbelievers were killed. One Muslim also embraced martyrdom. Plenty of war-spoils were also seized.

In the same battle, Umm al-Mu`mineen, Juwayriyah bint Harith was also among the captives. The Beloved Prophet صَلَّى اللهُ عَلَيْهِ وَاٰلِهٖ وَسَلَّم married her, and the Muslims released all the captives out of joy.

When the Beloved Prophet صَلَّى اللهُ عَلَيْهِ وَاٰلِهٖ وَسَلَّم was returning from this *ghazwah*, Sayyidatuna 'Aisha رَضِیَ اللهُ عَنْهَا was left behind at one place due to some reason. Later on, she joined the Final Messenger of Allah صَلَّى اللهُ عَلَيْهِ وَاٰلِهٖ وَسَلَّم. Making this a base, the hypocrites, مَعَاذَ الله, levelled false accusations against her. In the Holy Quran, Allah Almighty Himself mentioned the chastity of Sayyidatuna 'Aisha Siddiqah رَضِیَ اللهُ عَنْهَا in verses 11 to 20 of *Surah al-Noor*, and declared the accusations of the hypocrites to be a lie.

THE BATTLE OF THE TRENCH AND ITS CAUSE

The incident of "the Battle of the Trench" occurred in 5 Hijri. The Seal of the Prophets صَلَّى اللهُ عَلَيْهِ وَاٰلِهٖ وَسَلَّم had expelled the Jews of Banu Nadeer from Madinah due to their violation of the pacts. Some of them went to Khayber and settled there.

In Khayber, they formed an alliance with the local Jews and then incited the polytheists of Arabia to wage war against the Beloved Prophet صَلَّى اللهُ عَلَيْهِ وَاٰلِهٖ وَسَلَّم, ensuring them every kind of help and support from their end. All the disbelievers of Arabia formed a confederation and intended to go to war against the Muslims. For this reason, it is also called *Ghazwah al-Ahzaab* (the Battle of all the Confederates). The total number of the enemy was 10,000.

For this reason, Sayyiduna Salman Farsi رَضِیَ اللهُ عَنْهُ suggested: "It is better to engage in a defensive battle by staying inside the city. A trench should be dug on the side from where, there is a risk of disbelievers' invasion."

Since three sides of Madinah were surrounded by narrow streets of houses and clumps of date trees, hence, there was not any possibility of an invasion from those three sides. There was only one side that was open, therefore, it was decided that a deep trench should be dug on that side.

Therefore, on 8 Zul-Qa'dah of 5 Hijri, the Final Messenger of Allah صَلَّى اللّٰهُ عَلَيْهِ وَاٰلِهٖ وَسَلَّم engaged in digging the trench with 3,000 companions رَضِيَ اللّٰهُ عَنْهُم. He صَلَّى اللّٰهُ عَلَيْهِ وَاٰلِهٖ وَسَلَّم marked the boundaries of the trench with his own blessed hands, and distributed ten yards of land to ten men each. This trench was dug in approximately twenty days. The trench was 300 metres in length and 9 metres in width, whereas, the depth of the trench was 5 meters.

In that age, the use of a trench in a battle was a new experience for the people of Arabia, and it became one of the reasons for success in this battle. When the army of the disbelievers marched forward, they were astonished to see the trench before them. They besieged Madinah, and this siege lasted for approximately one month. This siege was so severe and tight that the Final Messenger of Allah صَلَّى اللّٰهُ عَلَيْهِ وَاٰلِهٖ وَسَلَّم and the blessed companions رَضِيَ اللّٰهُ عَنْهُم went without food completely on many occasions.

A few disbelievers crossed the trench from one place, but when their prominent warriors were killed, the remaining ones fled. In this battle, six Muslims embraced martyrdom. Abu Sufyan, who was the commander-in-chief of the army of the disbelievers at that time, got exasperated by the extremely cold weather, long siege and the military rations running out.

In this situation, Allah Almighty afflicted them with such a hurricane which put their cauldrons upside down and uprooted their tents. In short, they found themselves in such a situation where they had no other choice, but to flee.

The Battle of Banu Quraydhah

During the Battle of Trench, Banu Quraydhah broke the pact and helped the disbelievers. In order to punish them for this, the Beloved Prophet صَلَّى اللّٰهُ عَلَيْهِ وَاٰلِهٖ وَسَلَّم set out for Banu Quraydhah with his army immediately after the Battle of Trench. Banu Quraydhah surrendered after a siege of twenty-five days and said that whatever decision Sayyiduna Sa'd Bin Mu'aaz رَضِیَ اللّٰهُ عَنْهُ makes about them, they would accept it.

According to the decision made by Sayyiduna Sa'd رَضِیَ اللّٰهُ عَنْهُ, those who fought out of them were killed, their women and children were made prisoners, and their possessions were distributed among the *Mujahideen*.

Bear in mind that Banu Quraydhah themselves chose Sayyiduna Sa'd Bin Mu'aaz رَضِیَ اللّٰهُ عَنْهُ as a mediator and then his verdict was acted upon, and the decision of Sayyiduna Sa'd رَضِیَ اللّٰهُ عَنْهُ was actually in accordance with the religious teachings of Banu Quraydhah.

INTENTION OF 'UMRAH AND AN ASTONISHING MIRACLE

In the sixth year of migration, in Zul-Qa'dah, the Final Messenger of Allah صَلَّى اللّٰهُ عَلَيْهِ وَاٰلِهٖ وَسَلَّم set out for Makkah after wearing the *Ihram* of '*Umrah* with 1400 companions رَضِیَ اللّٰهُ عَنْهُم. He صَلَّى اللّٰهُ عَلَيْهِ وَاٰلِهٖ وَسَلَّم thought that the disbelievers of Makkah might stop them from performing the '*Umrah*, therefore, he صَلَّى اللّٰهُ عَلَيْهِ وَاٰلِهٖ وَسَلَّم had already sent a person from the Khuza'ah tribe to Makkah so that he could bring information about the intentions of the disbelievers of Makkah.

When the caravan of the Beloved Prophet صَلَّى اللّٰهُ عَلَيْهِ وَاٰلِهٖ وَسَلَّم reached near

‘Usfaan, he brought the news that the disbelievers of Makkah had gathered all the disbelievers of the Arab tribes and instructed them that they should not let the Muslims enter Makkah at any cost.

Therefore, the disbelievers of Makkah gathered all the tribes that were united with them and formed an army. In order to stop the Muslims, they went out of Makkah and camped at a place. The Final Messenger of Allah صَلَّى اللّٰهُ عَلَيْهِ وَاٰلِهٖ وَسَلَّم took a different path to where the army of disbelievers was deployed. Heading forward through an unusual path, the Muslims reached “Hudaybiyah”, and camped there.

There was a dire shortage of water in Hudaybiyah. There was only one well, which dried up in only a few hours. When the blessed companions became restless due to thirst, he صَلَّى اللّٰهُ عَلَيْهِ وَاٰلِهٖ وَسَلَّم placed his blessed hand into a large bowl, resulting in a water spring gushing forth from his blessed fingers.

He صَلَّى اللّٰهُ عَلَيْهِ وَاٰلِهٖ وَسَلَّم then poured the water he used for *Wudu* into the dry well along with one of his arrows. Due to this, so much water gushed out of the well that the entire Muslim army and all the animals continued to quench their thirst from that well for many days.

Hudaybiyah is a settlement, located approximately at the distance of 24 kilometres from Makkah. One part of it lies within the sacred precinct of the *Haram*, and one part of it lies outside the *Haram*. Nowadays, this place is known as Shumaysi.

BAY'AH al-Ridwan

After reaching Hudaybiyah, the Final Messenger of Allah صَلَّى اللّٰهُ عَلَيْهِ وَاٰلِهٖ وَسَلَّم saw that the disbelievers of Quraysh were ready for a war with their army, whereas, he صَلَّى اللّٰهُ عَلَيْهِ وَاٰلِهٖ وَسَلَّم and his companions were in the state of *Ihram*. He صَلَّى اللّٰهُ عَلَيْهِ وَاٰلِهٖ وَسَلَّم, therefore, thought it to be appropriate to hold peace talks with them. For this task, he صَلَّى اللّٰهُ عَلَيْهِ وَاٰلِهٖ وَسَلَّم sent Sayyiduna Uthman al-Ghani رَضِیَ اللّٰهُ عَنْهُ to Makkah.

So Sayyiduna Uthman رَضِیَ اللّٰهُ عَنْهُ went to Makkah and invited the disbelievers of Quraysh to make a peace treaty. The disbelievers said that we allow you to perform the *Tawaf* of the *Ka'bah*, and the

Sa'i of Safa and Marwah, but we would not let Muhammad (صَلَّى اللّٰهُ عَلَيْهِ وَاٰلِهٖ وَسَلَّم) enter the *Ka'bah* at all.

Sayyiduna Uthman رَضِیَ اللّٰهُ عَنْه said: "I will never perform '*Umrah* without the Final Messenger of Allah صَلَّى اللّٰهُ عَلَيْهِ وَاٰلِهٖ وَسَلَّم." The situation worsened and the disbelievers stopped him in Makkah.

This rumour spread in Hudaybiyah that the disbelievers of Quraysh have martyred Sayyiduna Uthman رَضِیَ اللّٰهُ عَنْه. When this news reached the Beloved Prophet صَلَّى اللّٰهُ عَلَيْهِ وَاٰلِهٖ وَسَلَّم, he صَلَّى اللّٰهُ عَلَيْهِ وَاٰلِهٖ وَسَلَّم said: "It is *fard* to take revenge for the blood of Uthman."

Having said this, he صَلَّى اللّٰهُ عَلَيْهِ وَاٰلِهٖ وَسَلَّم sat under a tree and said to the blessed companions رَضِیَ اللّٰهُ عَنْهُم: "Pledge allegiance on my hand that you will remain loyal to me until your last breath." All the companions pledged allegiance to him by taking this oath. This is the very same allegiance that is known as "*Bay'ah al-Ridwan*" in the history of Islam.

This tree and the allegiance pledged under it have been mentioned at two places in the Holy Quran—verse no. 7 of *Surah al-Ma'idah*, and in many verses of *Surah al-Fath*. After this pledge of allegiance, it was found out that the news of Sayyiduna Uthman's رَضِیَ اللّٰهُ عَنْه martyrdom was a false rumour. He was alive and perfectly fine.

Treaty of Hudaybiyah

and its Causes

The Final Messenger of Allah صَلَّى اللّٰهُ عَلَيْهِ وَاٰلِهٖ وَسَلَّم and his companions set out with the intention of performing '*Umrah*. For this reason, they also had sacrificial animals with them; but the disbelievers took oaths that they would not let the Muslims reach the blessed *Ka'bah* until they were alive.

When Sayyiduna Uthman al-Ghani رَضِیَ اللّٰهُ عَنْه took the message of the peace treaty from the Beloved Prophet صَلَّى اللهُ عَلَيْهِ وَاٰلِهٖ وَسَلَّم to Makkah, Quraysh also sent some people to him for talks, but nothing could be settled. Then Quraysh sent Suhail Bin 'Amr to set the conditions of the peace treaty, as a result of which, the Treaty of Hudaybiyah was formed. Some conditions of this treaty are as follows:

1. The Muslims shall return without performing *'Umrah* this year.
2. They can come for *'Umrah* next year, but they shall stay in Makkah for only three days.
3. There will be no fighting for the next ten years.
4. Arab tribes may have a friendship treaty with whichever tribe they want.
5. If any Muslim from Makkah goes to Madinah, it will be necessary to return him.

This peace treaty has been referred to as "*Fath Mubeen*" *(a clear victory)* in the Holy Quran. Outwardly, this treaty was against the Muslims, but the events occurring afterwards showed that this treaty became a key factor to the later achievements.

Chapter 10

After Hudaybiyah *to the* BLESSED APPARENT PASSING

Kings Invited to ISLAM

After the Treaty of Hudaybiyah, peace prevailed everywhere. Since the Final Messenger of Allah صَلَّى اللّٰهُ عَلَيْهِ وَاٰلِهٖ وَسَلَّم is the Prophet for the entire universe, hence, he صَلَّى اللّٰهُ عَلَيْهِ وَاٰلِهٖ وَسَلَّم intended to spread the message of Islam all over the world. Therefore, he صَلَّى اللّٰهُ عَلَيْهِ وَاٰلِهٖ وَسَلَّم sent letters to different kings through envoys. Its summary is as follows:

Name of the envoy	City/Country	King/Ameer	Reaction and Result
Sayyiduna Dihyah Kalbi	Bayt al-Muqaddas	Hiraql (Caesar of Rome)	He accepted Islam's veracity, but remained deprived of reciting the *Kalimah* due to his greed for the kingdom.[1]
Sayyiduna Abdullah bin Huzafah	Tesfoon	Kisra (Khusro Pervaiz)	Tore the letter; his son murdered him; his rule ended during the caliphate of Sayyiduna Umar رَضِیَ اللّٰهُ عَنْهُ.[2]
Sayyiduna 'Amr bin Umayyah	Aksoom	Ash'amah Najjashi	Showed great respect to the letter and embraced Islam.[3]
Sayyiduna Haatib bin Abi Balta'a	Alexandria	Muqawqas (King of Egypt)	Showed great respect to the letter, but did not embrace Islam; sent precious gifts to the Beloved Prophet.[4]

1 Bukhari, chapter 6, vol. 1, p. 12, Hadith 7, summarised
2 Subul-al-Huda war-rashad, vol. 11, p. 362, summarised
3 Subul-al-Huda war-rashad, vol. 11, p. 365, summarised
4 Subul-al-Huda war-rashad, vol. 11, p. 348-349, summarised

Sayyiduna 'Ala bin Hadrami	Bahrain	Mundhir bin Saawa	Showed great respect to the letter and embraced Islam with majority of the people of his nation.[1]
Sayyiduna 'Amr bin 'Aas	Oman	Two sons of Julandi—Jafar and 'Abd	Showed great respect to the letter; both of them embraced Islam.[2]
Sayyiduna Sulayt bin 'Amr	Yamamah	Hauza bin Ali	Showed great respect to the letter; also respected the envoy, but conditioned his acceptance of Islam upon being given rulership, which was not accepted.[3]
Sayyiduna Shuja' bin Wahb	Ghutah (Damascus)	Harith bin Abi Shamir Ghasani	This arrogant person became angry after reading the letter and ordered his army to be ready, resulting in the battles like "The Battle of Mu'tah" and "The Battle of Tabuk" taking place.[4]

The Battle of Khayber and its causes

The Battle of Khayber was fought in Muharram al-Haraam. According to one opinion, it occurred in 7 Hijri.

Khayber was the biggest centre of the Jews in Arabia. The Jews of Khayber were very rich and wealthy, and were experts in warfare.

1 Sharh al-Zurqaani 'Ala-Al-Mawahib, vol. 5, pp. 34-36, summarised
2 Subul-ul-Huda war-rashad, vol. 5, pp. 37-43, selected
3 Madarij-un-Nubuwwah, vol. 2, p. 228-229, summarised
4 Subul-ul-Huda war-rashad, vol. 11, pp. 358-359, summarised | Seerat-e-Mustafa, p. 373

They had built many strong forts there, eight out of which are very famous. The combination of these eight forts is called "Khayber".[1]

The Jews of Khayber were at the forefront of the disbelievers who attacked Madinah in the Battle of Trench. They were the ones who intensified this battle and laid the foundation of this war. It was them who incited the disbelievers of Makkah to invade Madinah and also helped them financially. The disgrace and humiliation faced in the Battle of Trench made them further grieved and furious. Uniting with other tribes, they started conspiring to invade Madinah again.[2]

When the Final Messenger of Allah صَلَّى اللّٰهُ عَلَيْهِ وَاٰلِهٖ وَسَلَّم came to know about their conspiracies, he صَلَّى اللّٰهُ عَلَيْهِ وَاٰلِهٖ وَسَلَّم left for Khayber with an army of 1,600 companions رَضِىَ اللّٰهُ عَنْهُم.[3]

1 Sharh Al-Zurqaani 'ala al-Mawahib,, vol. 3, p. 243, selected

2 Seerat-e-Mustafa, p. 381, summarised

3 Khayber is situated to the north of Madinah on the way to Tabuk. It is at a distance of around 153 kilometres from Madinah. The land of Khayber was fertile and the area was known for the fine produce of dates. There were so many orchards there that the city was not visible. Now, the new city is situated away from the ancient area.

The Beloved Prophet صَلَّى اللّٰهُ عَلَيْهِ وَاٰلِهٖ وَسَلَّم entered the boundaries of Khayber in the night. It was his blessed habit that he صَلَّى اللّٰهُ عَلَيْهِ وَاٰلِهٖ وَسَلَّم would not attack any nation in the night.

He صَلَّى اللّٰهُ عَلَيْهِ وَاٰلِهٖ وَسَلَّم entered the city after *Fajr Salah*. The Jews made a plan to fight staying inside the forts. All the forts were gradually conquered. The biggest and strongest fort of Khayber was 'Qamoos', which was conquered by Sayyiduna Ali رَضِیَ اللّٰهُ عَنْهُ. Ninety-three Jews were killed in the battles which took place in Khayber, whereas, fifteen companions رَضِیَ اللّٰهُ عَنْهُم embraced martyrdom.[1]

After the conquest, the Jews requested not to be expelled from Khayber, and that their land should also be left under their possession. In exchange, half of the produce should be taken from them.

The Final Messenger of Allah صَلَّى اللّٰهُ عَلَيْهِ وَاٰلِهٖ وَسَلَّم accepted their request. When the produce was ready, the Beloved Prophet صَلَّى اللّٰهُ عَلَيْهِ وَاٰلِهٖ وَسَلَّم sent Sayyiduna Abdullah Bin Rawahah رَضِیَ اللّٰهُ عَنْهُ to divide it. He divided it equally into two parts and said to the Jews to take whatever part they wanted.

Surprised at the distribution, they said: "The earth and the sky exist due to this justice."[2]

Alongside the conquest of Khayber, many other areas were also conquered. A war was fought at some places, and some areas were conquered without any war.[3]

1 Sharh al-Zurqaani 'ala al-Mawahib, vol. 3, p. 352-353, selected
2 Futooh al-Buldaan, pp. 33-35, selected
3 Sharh al-Zurqaani 'ala al-Mawahib, vol. 3, p. 303, summarised

Performed Qada Umrah

One of the conditions of the peace treaty which was made at Hudaybiyah was that Muslims would perform '*Umrah* the next year and would stay in Makkah for three days. Upon the completion of one year, in Zul-Qa'dah of 7 Hijri, the Final Messenger of Allah صَلَّى اللّٰهُ عَلَيْهِ وَاٰلِهٖ وَسَلَّم announced: "All those who were present in Hudaybiyah last year should come."

All the companions, except the martyred ones, attained this privilege. The Beloved Prophet صَلَّى اللّٰهُ عَلَيْهِ وَاٰلِهٖ وَسَلَّم set out for Makkah with two thousand Muslims. Sixty camels were also with them for sacrifice.[1]

When the Final Messenger of Allah صَلَّى اللّٰهُ عَلَيْهِ وَاٰلِهٖ وَسَلَّم entered the sanctuary of Makkah, some disbelievers were observing this scene by climbing up the nearby mountains. They said to each other: "How will they perform *Tawaf*? Hunger and fever have weakened them."

---

1 Sharh al-Zurqaani 'ala al-Mawahib, vol. 3, p. 314, summarised

Reaching the sanctuary of Makkah, the Beloved Prophet صَلَّى اللّٰهُ عَلَيْهِ وَاٰلِهٖ وَسَلَّم wore his shawl in such a way that left his right arm and shoulder uncovered.[1] He صَلَّى اللّٰهُ عَلَيْهِ وَاٰلِهٖ وَسَلَّم then said:" May Allah shower His mercy upon the one who shows his power before these disbelievers."

Then, along with his companions, he صَلَّى اللّٰهُ عَلَيْهِ وَاٰلِهٖ وَسَلَّم performed the first three rounds of *Tawaf* very firmly by moving his shoulders, and with a great pride.[2] This Sunnah still exists today. Every *Tawaf*-performing person acts upon it in the first three rounds.

Then the Beloved Prophet صَلَّى اللّٰهُ عَلَيْهِ وَاٰلِهٖ وَسَلَّم performed the *Sa'i* of Safa and Marwah, and slaughtered the sacrificial animals. He صَلَّى اللّٰهُ عَلَيْهِ وَاٰلِهٖ وَسَلَّم remained in Makkah for three days and then returned to Madinah. Since this *'Umr*ah was due to the *'Um*rah of the previous year, that is why it is called *'Umrah-tul-Qada.*[3]

Causes of the Battle of Mu'tah

"Mu'tah" is a place in the Levant. The cause of this battle is as follows:

The Final Messenger of Allah صَلَّى اللّٰهُ عَلَيْهِ وَاٰلِهٖ وَسَلَّم wrote a letter to Qayser, the king of Busra[4], and sent it through Sayyiduna Harith Bin Umair رَضِىَ اللّٰهُ عَنْهُ. On the way, Sharahbeel Bin 'Amr martyred him. When this news reached the Beloved Prophet صَلَّى اللّٰهُ عَلَيْهِ وَاٰلِهٖ وَسَلَّم, it deeply grieved him. At that time, he صَلَّى اللّٰهُ عَلَيْهِ وَاٰلِهٖ وَسَلَّم mobilised an army of 3,000 Muslims, and tying a white flag with his own blessed hands, handed it to Sayyiduna Zaid bin Haarithah رَضِىَ اللّٰهُ عَنْهُ, appointing him

1 It is called Idtiba.

2 It is called ***"Ramal"*** in Arabic.

3 Sharh al-Zurqaani 'ala al-Mawahib, vol. 3, pg. 315-325

4 ***Busra:*** It is the area of the Levant, where at that time, Shurahbeel Bin 'Amr was the governor. He would pay tributes to Caesar, the king of Rome. Remember! Busra and Basra are the names of two different cities. The city Basra was inhabited as barracks by Sayyiduna Umar رَضِىَ اللّٰهُ عَنْهُ during his caliphate.

the commander-in-chief of the army. In addition, he صَلَّى اللهُ عَلَيْهِ وَاٰلِهٖ وَسَلَّم also said: "If he is martyred, then Ja'far Bin Abu Taalib will be the chief. If he is martyred, then Abdullah Bin Rawahah will be the chief."[1]

The Battle of Mu'tah

When this army set out under the leadership of Sayyiduna Zaid رَضِیَ اللهُ عَنْهُ, they were given the news that Caesar of Rome was there himself with one hundred thousand soldiers. A further one hundred thousand Christian Arabs were also joining him.

The field of Mu'tah where the Battle of Mu'tah took place

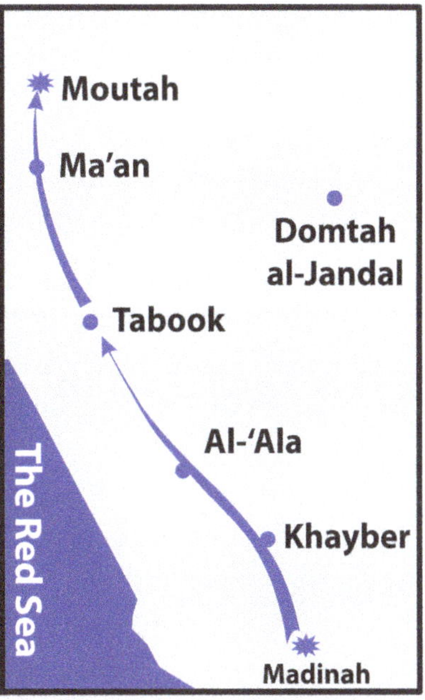

Mu'tah is the area between Karak, a city of modern-day Jordan, and the Jordan River. Jordan is a country in Western Asia, and Amman is its capital. At that time, the people of the Levant ruled there. It was the first time that the army of Muslims went so far away from Madinah for a battle. The distance between Jordan and Madinah is at least more than one thousand kilometres.

1 Sharh al-Zurqaani 'ala al-Mawahib, vol. 3, pp. 339-342

Sayyiduna Zaid consulted about whether he should write a letter to the Final Messenger of Allah صَلَّى اللّٰهُ عَلَيْهِ وَاٰلِهٖ وَسَلَّم, requesting for more soldiers, or should he start the battle. Sayyiduna Abdullah Bin Rawahah رَضِیَ اللّٰهُ عَنْهُ said: "Our purpose is not victory or wealth, rather, our purpose is martyrdom."

Having heard this, people said: "Abdullah has spoken the truth." Then, they moved forward and camped at Mu'tah. The army was organized and the whole army was ready for the battle.

An astonishing battle in the history of the mankind took place here where an army of two hundred thousand was fighting against only three thousand devoted warriors.

According to the foretelling of the Final Messenger of Allah صَلَّى اللّٰهُ عَلَيْهِ وَاٰلِهٖ وَسَلَّم, Sayyiduna Zaid رَضِیَ اللّٰهُ عَنْهُ was martyred. When Sayyiduna Zaid رَضِیَ اللّٰهُ عَنْهُ was martyred, then Sayyiduna Ja'far رَضِیَ اللّٰهُ عَنْهُ held the flag of Islam, and when he was martyred, Sayyiduna Abdullah Bin Rawahah رَضِیَ اللّٰهُ عَنْهُ held the flag. The Beloved Prophet صَلَّى اللّٰهُ عَلَيْهِ وَاٰلِهٖ وَسَلَّم was observing all these incidents in Madinah and mentioning them.[1]

After the martyrdom of Sayyiduna Abdullah Bin Rawahah رَضِیَ اللّٰهُ عَنْهُ, Sayyiduna Khalid Bin Waleed رَضِیَ اللّٰهُ عَنْهُ held the flag and fought so bravely that nine swords broke in his hand. With excellent war skills and expertise, he took out the Islamic army from the siege of the enemy and brought them back to Madinah. It was a victory for the Muslims as only twelve companions رَضِیَ اللّٰهُ عَنْهُم were martyred against the army of one hundred thousand soldiers[2]. The remaining Muslim army returned safe and sound, whereas, the enemy suffered a far greater loss than this.[3]

---

1 Sharh al-Zurqaani 'ala al-Mawahib, vol. 3, pp. 344-347, summarised

2 According to some narrations, the number of the army of disbelievers was two hundred thousand. This battle continued for seven days, and it has been stated that twenty thousand soldiers of the enemy were killed, whereas, only twelve companions were martyred.

3 Sharh al-Zurqaani 'ala al-Mawahib, vol. 3, pp. 348-349, summarised

CAUSES OF THE CONQUEST of MAKKAH

According to the treaty made in Hudaybiyah, there was a ceasefire agreement between the Muslims and the disbelievers of Quraysh for ten years. In the light of this treaty, the tribe Banu Bakr formed an alliance with Quraysh, and Banu Khaza'ah were joined (in alliance) with Muslims. There had been enmity between both these tribes for a long time.

Once, Banu Bakr along with Quraysh, attacked the ally of Muslims, Banu Khaza'ah. The people of Banu Khaza'ah entered the sanctuary of the *Ka'bah* to save their lives, but they were not spared even there. Twenty-three people of Banu Khaza'ah were killed in this attack. Banu Khaza'ah requested the Beloved Prophet صَلَّى اللّٰهُ عَلَيْهِ وَاٰلِهٖ وَسَلَّم for help.[1]

He صَلَّى اللّٰهُ عَلَيْهِ وَاٰلِهٖ وَسَلَّم sent a message to Quraysh saying: "Accept any one of the (following) three things:

1. Pay blood money of the killed people!
2. Or terminate the alliance with Banu Bakr!
3. Or make the announcement that the Treaty of Hudaybiyah has been ended."

Having heard these conditions, the representative of Quraysh announced the decision to end the treaty. As soon as the envoy of the Final Messenger of Allah صَلَّى اللّٰهُ عَلَيْهِ وَاٰلِهٖ وَسَلَّم left, Quraysh realized that they had made a very big mistake. They immediately sent Abu Sufyan to Madinah in order to form a new treaty like before, but he was paid no attention.

Disappointed, Abu Sufyan announced the renewal of the treaty by standing in Masjid al-Nabawi himself, but no one responded to him. He went to Makkah and mentioned the entire situation to the chiefs of Quraysh.

They asked him: "Did they respond to your announcement?" To which, Abu Sufyan replied: "No." The disbelievers of Quraysh said: "It is nothing then; it is neither a peace treaty so that we can be relaxed, nor is it a declaration of war so that we may prepare for it."

In the meanwhile, the Final Messenger of Allah صَلَّى اللّٰهُ عَلَيْهِ وَاٰلِهٖ وَسَلَّم prepared for the battle very secretly. The purpose behind it was that the people of Makkah should not get to know about it and they should be attacked when they are unaware of it.[2]

---

1 Sharh al-Zurqaani 'Ala al-Mawahib vol. 3, p. 276-380, summarised

2 Sharh al-Zurqaani 'Ala al-Mawahib vol. 3, p. 384-386, selected and summarised

BELOVED PROPHET'S ENTRY INTO MAKKAH

In the 8th year of migration, on 10th of Ramadan, the Final Messenger of Allah صَلَّى اللّٰهُ عَلَيْهِ وَاٰلِهٖ وَسَلَّم left for Makkah with an army of approx. 10,000 warriors. Some tribes joined him on the way, making the number of the army 12,000.[1]

Before entering Makkah, he صَلَّى اللّٰهُ عَلَيْهِ وَاٰلِهٖ وَسَلَّم divided the army into two parts. In one part, he صَلَّى اللّٰهُ عَلَيْهِ وَاٰلِهٖ وَسَلَّم was present himself, whereas the second part was given under the command of Sayyiduna Khalid bin Waleed رَضِیَ اللّٰهُ عَنْهُ, and he was ordered to enter Makkah following the other route.[2]

As soon as the Beloved Prophet صَلَّى اللّٰهُ عَلَيْهِ وَاٰلِهٖ وَسَلَّم reached the land of Makkah, the first order that he issued was as follows:

- The one who surrenders is ensured protection.
- The one who shuts his door is ensured protection.
- The one who enters the *Ka'bah* is ensured protection.
- The one who enters the house of Abu Sufyan is ensured protection.[3]

This merciful announcement of the Beloved Prophet صَلَّى اللّٰهُ عَلَيْهِ وَاٰلِهٖ وَسَلَّم created a peaceful environment everywhere. There was not any possibility left for even a drop of blood to be shed, but some people of Quraysh attacked the army of Sayyiduna Khalid Bin Waleed رَضِیَ اللّٰهُ عَنْهُ, resulting in three Muslims being martyred, and approximately twelve disbelievers being killed.

When the Beloved Prophet صَلَّى اللّٰهُ عَلَيْهِ وَاٰلِهٖ وَسَلَّم saw that swords are being used and arrows are being fired, he صَلَّى اللّٰهُ عَلَيْهِ وَاٰلِهٖ وَسَلَّم asked: "Why

1 Sharh al-Zurqaani 'Ala al-Mawahib vol. 3, p. 395, summarised
2 Bukhari, vol. 3, p. 102, Hadith 4280
3 Sharh al-Zurqaani 'Ala al-Mawahib vol. 3, p. 417-422, summarised

are swords being used despite forbidding from a war?" It was humbly replied: "The disbelievers started it." The Beloved Prophet صَلَّى اللّٰهُ عَلَيْهِ وَاٰلِهٖ وَسَلَّم said: "The Lord Almighty has sealed the fate. Whatever Allah عَزَّوَجَلَّ willed is better."[1]

The Final Messenger of Allah صَلَّى اللّٰهُ عَلَيْهِ وَاٰلِهٖ وَسَلَّم became the conqueror of Makkah, but the state of his humility was such that he صَلَّى اللّٰهُ عَلَيْهِ وَاٰلِهٖ وَسَلَّم was sat upon his (she-)camel reciting the blessed verses of *Surah al-Fath* with his blessed head lowered in a way that it was touching the saddle of his camel.[2]

He صَلَّى اللّٰهُ عَلَيْهِ وَاٰلِهٖ وَسَلَّم made his (she-) camel sit, performed *Tawaf* and kissed the *Hajr al-Aswad*. Then, he صَلَّى اللّٰهُ عَلَيْهِ وَاٰلِهٖ وَسَلَّم commanded for all the idols to be removed from the *Ka'bah*. When all the idols were removed from the holy *Ka'bah*, he صَلَّى اللّٰهُ عَلَيْهِ وَاٰلِهٖ وَسَلَّم went inside, recited *Takbeer* in every corner of the *Ka'bah*, and offered two *Rak'ah Salah* there.[3]

1 Sharh al-Zurqaani 'Ala al-Mawahib vol. 3, p. 416-417, summarised
2 Sharh al-Zurqaani 'Ala al-Mawahib vol. 3, p. 434, summarised
3 Bukhari, vol. 3, p. 102, Hadith 4288, summarised

MERCIFUL BEHAVIOUR *of the* Beloved Prophet ﷺ

After this, the Beloved Prophet صَلَّى اللّٰهُ عَلَيْهِ وَاٰلِهٖ وَسَلَّم held a (first) public court in the sanctuary (Haram) around the *Ka'bah* where along with the Muslim troops, thousands of disbelievers were also present. Amongst these disbelievers were the people who had persecuted the Beloved Prophet صَلَّى اللّٰهُ عَلَيْهِ وَاٰلِهٖ وَسَلَّم and his blessed companions greatly, placed thorns in his path, threw impurities on his blessed body, made attempts to assassinate him, martyred his blessed companions, forced him to leave Makkah, levelled false accusations against him and called him names. In short, they committed every type of brutality.

Now, they all were standing as criminals before the Beloved Prophet صَلَّى اللّٰهُ عَلَيْهِ وَاٰلِهٖ وَسَلَّم. If he صَلَّى اللّٰهُ عَلَيْهِ وَاٰلِهٖ وَسَلَّم had wanted, he could have taken severe revenge on them, but he صَلَّى اللّٰهُ عَلَيْهِ وَاٰلِهٖ وَسَلَّم did not take any revenge whatsoever. Rather, he صَلَّى اللّٰهُ عَلَيْهِ وَاٰلِهٖ وَسَلَّم said in his merciful tone: لَا تَثْرِيْبَ عَلَيْكُمُ الْيَوْمَ فَاذْهَبُوْا اَنْتُمُ الطُّلَقَآءُ "*Today, there is no blame on you. Go! You all are free.*"[1]

Treating well the enemies who tortured the Beloved Prophet صَلَّى اللّٰهُ عَلَيْهِ وَاٰلِهٖ وَسَلَّم and his blessed companions in different ways after having a victory over them is something the example of which cannot be found.

On the second day of the conquest of Makkah, the Beloved Prophet صَلَّى اللّٰهُ عَلَيْهِ وَاٰلِهٖ وَسَلَّم delivered another sermon in which the rulings on the sanctuary around the *Ka'bah* were mentioned and battle and fighting in this sanctuary was declared as forbidden forever.

On this occasion, by virtue of his good treatment, a large number of people embraced Islam. He صَلَّى اللّٰهُ عَلَيْهِ وَاٰلِهٖ وَسَلَّم had the other idols (present around Makkah) destroyed.[2]

---

1 Sharh al-Zurqaani 'Ala al-Mawahib vol. 3, p. 449, summarised
2 Sharh al-Zurqaani 'Ala al-Mawahib vol. 3, pp. 487-490, selected

The Battle of Hunayn

Due to the conquest of Makkah, it became apparent to the entire Arabian Peninsula that Islam was true. In this way, many tribes started embracing Islam. But after this news, the people of the Hawazin tribe, together with other few small tribes, set out with the intention to attack the Muslims.

When the last Prophet of Allah صَلَّى اللّٰهُ عَلَيْهِ وَاٰلِهٖ وَسَلَّم learnt about it, he صَلَّى اللّٰهُ عَلَيْهِ وَاٰلِهٖ وَسَلَّم set out with 12,000 soldiers. The Islamic army faced the disbelievers at *Hunayn*[1] which is situated between Makkah and Taif. In the beginning, the Muslims fought skilfully and attacked in such a way that the army of disbelievers started fleeing from the battlefield, but when their troops that were waiting in ambush attacked, the Islamic army fell into panic. In the end, it was the Muslims who prevailed and, in this battle, they captured thousands of prisoners and seized large amounts of spoils of war.[2]

After this, the Last Prophet of Allah صَلَّى اللّٰهُ عَلَيْهِ وَاٰلِهٖ وَسَلَّم set out for Taif and besieged the fort of Taif. The siege lasted more than two weeks, but it did not benefit much, so he صَلَّى اللّٰهُ عَلَيْهِ وَاٰلِهٖ وَسَلَّم ordered for the siege to end and made Du'a: "O Allah! Give guidance to Thaqeef, i.e. the people of Taif."

By virtue of the Du'a of the Beloved Prophet صَلَّى اللّٰهُ عَلَيْهِ وَاٰلِهٖ وَسَلَّم, the people of Taif became Muslim in 9 Hijri. At their request, all the prisoners were released. On returning from Taif, the Beloved Prophet صَلَّى اللّٰهُ عَلَيْهِ وَاٰلِهٖ وَسَلَّم distributed the spoils of war gained from the Battle of Hunayn amongst the Muslims. He صَلَّى اللّٰهُ عَلَيْهِ وَاٰلِهٖ وَسَلَّم stayed in Makkah for more than two weeks and then returned to Madinah.[3]

---

1 Hunayn is a valley which is at a distance of approximately 29 km from Makkah and 462 km from Madinah.

2 Sharh al-Zurqaani 'Ala al-Mawahib vol. 3, pp. 496-531, selected and summarised

3 Sharh al-Zurqaani 'Ala al-Mawahib vol. 4, pp. 6-19, selected and summarised

The Battle of Tabuk

In the 9th year of migration, in Rajab, the Battle of Tabuk took place. There is a place between Madinah and the Levant named "Tabuk". It is also called *Jaysh al-Usra* (i.e. army with insufficient provisions).[1]

Masjid at-Taubah situated in Tabuk

The city of Tabuk is at a distance of 552 km from Madinah. The distance by road is approximately 682 km. The place where the Muslim army camped is known today by the name of 'the Fort of Tabuk'. This was the final battle in which the Beloved Prophet صَلَّى اللّٰهُ عَلَيْهِ وَاٰلِهٖ وَسَلَّم participated physically.

1 Sharh al-Zurqaani 'Ala al-Mawahib, vol. 4, p. 65, summarised

It was instigated when the news reached Madinah that the Romans and the Arab Christians had prepared a big army in order to attack Madinah. In order to combat them, the Final Messenger of Allah صَلَّى اللّٰهُ عَلَيْهِ وَاٰلِهٖ وَسَلَّم issued an order to prepare an army. At that time, a severe famine had struck the entire Hijaz region and the weather was extremely hot too, such that it was very difficult for people to even come out of their homes.

It is this battle, Sayyiduna Abu Bakr رَضِىَ اللّٰهُ عَنْهُ presented all the belongings of his home and Sayyiduna Umar رَضِىَ اللّٰهُ عَنْهُ presented half of the belongings of his home in order to equip the army.[1] Sayyiduna Uthman al-Ghani رَضِىَ اللّٰهُ عَنْهُ and Sayyiduna Abd al-Rahman Bin 'Auf رَضِىَ اللّٰهُ عَنْهُ gave special support in this regard.

The Beloved Prophet صَلَّى اللّٰهُ عَلَيْهِ وَاٰلِهٖ وَسَلَّم set out for Tabuk with an army of 30,000 troops. Having reached Tabuk, he صَلَّى اللّٰهُ عَلَيْهِ وَاٰلِهٖ وَسَلَّم ordered the army to camp there. There was no sign of the Roman army even at a distance. Then, it was learnt that when spies informed Caesar about the glory and dignity of the Islamic army and their number, out of awe and fear, they lost courage for the battle and could not come out of their homes. The Final Messenger of Allah صَلَّى اللّٰهُ عَلَيْهِ وَاٰلِهٖ وَسَلَّم stayed in Tabuk for 20 days and then returned to Madinah. Tabuk and some nearby areas were included in the Islamic empire.[2]

Sayyiduna Abu Bakr Siddeeq AS AMEER OF HAJJ

In the 9th year of migration, in Zul Qa'dah, after returning from the Battle of Tabuk, the Final Messenger of Allah صَلَّى اللّٰهُ عَلَيْهِ وَاٰلِهٖ وَسَلَّم sent a caravan of 300 Muslims to Makkah for Hajj. Sayyiduna Abu Bakr Siddeeq رَضِىَ اللّٰهُ عَنْهُ was appointed the *Ameer* of Hajj, Sayyiduna Ali Murtaza رَضِىَ اللّٰهُ عَنْهُ the *Naqeeb* of Islam and Sayyiduna Sa'd Bin Abi Waqas, Sayyiduna Jabir Bin Abdullah and Sayyiduna Abu Hurayrah رَضِىَ اللّٰهُ عَنْهُم were appointed the teachers.

1 Tirmizi, vol. 5, p. 380, Hadith 3695

2 Madarij-un-Nubuwwah, vol. 2, p. 349, summarised

He صَلَّى اللّٰهُ عَلَيْهِ وَاٰلِهٖ وَسَلَّم also sent twenty camels on his own behalf for sacrifice. Sayyiduna Abu Bakr Siddeeq رَضِیَ اللّٰهُ عَنْهُ delivered a sermon in the sanctuary around the *Ka'bah* as well as at Arafat and Mina. Sayyiduna Ali رَضِیَ اللّٰهُ عَنْهُ stood up and recited forty verses of *Surah al-Bara`ah* and announced: "From now onwards, no polytheist can enter the *Ka'bah* nor can anyone perform *Tawaf* naked.[1] After four months, protection will be ended for disbelievers and polytheists."

Sayyiduna Abu Hurayrah and other blessed companions رَضِیَ اللّٰهُ عَنْهُم made the announcements so loudly that they lost their voices. After these announcements, people came in droves and became Muslim.

Arrival of delegations

9 Hijri is also called the year of delegations (*Wufood*). '*Wufood*' is the plural form of '*Wafd*' in Arabic. A '*Wafd*' is a group of more than one person. The Final Messenger of Allah صَلَّى اللّٰهُ عَلَيْهِ وَاٰلِهٖ وَسَلَّم would send preachers everywhere for preaching Islam. Some people would become Muslim after accepting the invitation of Islam at the hands of these preachers, whereas some tribes would desire to go directly to the Prophetic court to witness the beauty of Prophethood and express their Islam.

For this reason, some people would come to Madinah as representatives of their tribes and would embrace Islam after listening to the message of the invitation to Islam from the founder of Islam himself, the Final Messenger of Allah صَلَّى اللّٰهُ عَلَيْهِ وَاٰلِهٖ وَسَلَّم. Then they would go back to their tribes and make them Muslim.

Such kind of delegations had been coming to Madinah at different times, but after the conquest of Makkah, the flag of Islam had been raised in the entire Arabian Peninsula.

1 Sharh al-Zurqaani 'Ala al-Mawahib vol. 4, p. 115-116, summarised & Bukhari, vol. 3, p. 128, Hadith 4363

The Reason for the Abundance of Delegations

Many tribes had already accepted the truth about Islam, but they could not embrace Islam due to the fear of and pressure from the Quraysh. The Conquest of Makkah removed this obstacle. Now, the teachings of Islam and the sacred message of the Holy Quran ruled all hearts such that those who could not even bear to hear anything about Islam began to now sacrifice themselves at the blessed feet of the Prophet صَلَّى اللّٰهُ عَلَيْهِ وَاٰلِهٖ وَسَلَّم.

Impressed by the teachings and character of the true Prophet, these people would now come to him in large numbers from far and wide as delegations to embrace Islam and to be crowned with the honour of being from his blessed companions, thus attaining everlasting felicity.

In 9 Hijri after the conquest of Makkah, so many delegations came that the year was named 'سَنَةُ الْوُفُود' i.e. the year of the arrival of delegations. According to one opinion, approximately sixty delegations came to the Beloved Prophet صَلَّى اللّٰهُ عَلَيْهِ وَاٰلِهٖ وَسَلَّم that year.

He صَلَّى اللّٰهُ عَلَيْهِ وَاٰلِهٖ وَسَلَّم would make special arrangements for welcoming and meeting the delegations of tribes. For every delegation, he صَلَّى اللّٰهُ عَلَيْهِ وَاٰلِهٖ وَسَلَّم would come in very nice clothes and sit leaning against a pillar in Masjid al-Nabawi in order to meet them. Then, he صَلَّى اللّٰهُ عَلَيْهِ وَاٰلِهٖ وَسَلَّم would converse cheerfully with every delegation and educate them about essential beliefs and commandments of Islam. He صَلَّى اللّٰهُ عَلَيْهِ وَاٰلِهٖ وَسَلَّم would accommodate those guests in the best houses, take special care of their hospitality and would also give gifts to every delegation.

Delegation of Kindah

One of these delegations is the delegation of Kindah. These people lived in the surroundings of Yemen. Seventy to eighty people of this tribe came to Madinah with great splendour. With combed hair, in silk robes, and with weapons adorned on their bodies, they entered Madinah. When these people came to the Beloved Prophet صَلَّى اللّٰهُ عَلَيْهِ وَاٰلِهٖ وَسَلَّم, he صَلَّى اللّٰهُ عَلَيْهِ وَاٰلِهٖ وَسَلَّم asked: "Have you embraced Islam?" All of them replied in the affirmative. He صَلَّى اللّٰهُ عَلَيْهِ وَاٰلِهٖ وَسَلَّم said: "Then, why are you wearing silk clothes?" As soon as they heard this, they took off silk robes and also tore off the remaining pieces of silk from their clothes.

Delegation of Fazarah

One of the delegations was the delegation of Fazarah. It was a delegation of twenty people. They came and announced that they embraced Islam and said to the Beloved Prophet صَلَّى اللّٰهُ عَلَيْهِ وَاٰلِهٖ وَسَلَّم: "There is a severe famine in our area. Now, it is unbearable for us to face poverty and hunger. Please have mercy and make Du'a for rain."

The last Prophet of Allah صَلَّى اللّٰهُ عَلَيْهِ وَاٰلِهٖ وَسَلَّم made a Du'a on the pulpit on Friday. The rain started falling immediately and continued to fall for an entire week. On the next Friday, when the Final Messenger of Allah صَلَّى اللّٰهُ عَلَيْهِ وَاٰلِهٖ وَسَلَّم was delivering the sermon, an Arab villager humbly said: "O Messenger of Allah صَلَّى اللّٰهُ عَلَيْهِ وَاٰلِهٖ وَسَلَّم! Due to abundant rain, our cattle have started dying; our family members are restless due to hunger and all the roads have been blocked. Please make Du'a that this rain falls on the mountains and not on the fields."

The Beloved Prophet صَلَّى اللهُ عَلَيْهِ وَاٰلِهٖ وَسَلَّم made Du'a. When he صَلَّى اللهُ عَلَيْهِ وَاٰلِهٖ وَسَلَّم made the Du'a, the clouds moved away from Madinah. In this way, the sun appeared in Madinah after eight days.

Delegation of the Sa'd Bin Bakr tribe

One of the delegations came with Sayyiduna Damam Bin Tha'labah رَضِىَ اللهُ عَنْهُ, the chief of the Sa'd Bin Bakr tribe. He was a very handsome man with a rosy complexion and long hair. He came to the Final Messenger of Allah صَلَّى اللهُ عَلَيْهِ وَاٰلِهٖ وَسَلَّم and said: "O son of Abdul Muttalib! I will ask you questions about a few things and I will be harsh in the questions. Do not get displeased with me."

The Beloved Prophet صَلَّى اللهُ عَلَيْهِ وَاٰلِهٖ وَسَلَّم replied: "Whatever you want, you can ask from me." Then, the conversation took place like this:

Damam bin Tha'labah: By oath to the God Who is your Lord and the Lord of all humans, I ask: Has Allah Almighty sent you to us after making you His messenger?

The Beloved Prophet ﷺ: Yes.

Damam bin Tha'labah: By oath to God, I ask the question: Has Allah Almighty made *Salah*, fasting, *Hajj* and *Zakah* obligatory for us?

The Beloved Prophet ﷺ: Yes.

Damam Bin Tha'labah: Whatever you have said, I believe in it and I am Damam Bin Tha'labah. My tribe has sent me to you so that I can understand your religion very well and then convey the message of Islam to my tribe, Bani Sa'd bin Bakr.

He then reached his homeland and gathered his entire tribe. First, he condemned the idols and then delivered such an excellent speech on the truthfulness of Islam that all the men and women of the tribe became Muslim overnight. They broke the idols into pieces with their own hands, had a *Masjid* built in their tribe and became firm believers who acted upon the commandments of Islam.

Many other delegations also came to the Beloved Prophet صَلَّى اللهُ عَلَيْهِ وَاٰلِهٖ وَسَلَّم and embraced Islam.

Farewell Hajj

(*Hajja-tul-Wada'*)

The most important incident of the 10th year of the migration is the Farewell Hajj. It was the last Hajj of the Beloved Prophet صَلَّى اللهُ عَلَيْهِ وَاٰلِهٖ وَسَلَّم. People witnessed him performing the complete *Hajj*. In Zul Qa'dah, he صَلَّى اللهُ عَلَيْهِ وَاٰلِهٖ وَسَلَّم announced that he would set out for *Hajj*. During this *Hajj*, he صَلَّى اللهُ عَلَيْهِ وَاٰلِهٖ وَسَلَّم delivered his famous farewell sermon.

As the Final Messenger of Allah صَلَّى اللهُ عَلَيْهِ وَاٰلِهٖ وَسَلَّم announced that he would perform Hajj, approximately 124,000 of his devotees gathered around him. He صَلَّى اللهُ عَلَيْهِ وَاٰلِهٖ وَسَلَّم also indicated towards his apparent veiling from this world during this *Hajj* when, near the Jamarat, he صَلَّى اللهُ عَلَيْهِ وَاٰلِهٖ وَسَلَّم said: "Learn the rulings of *Hajj* from me! Perhaps after this, I will not perform another Hajj."

He صَلَّى اللهُ عَلَيْهِ وَاٰلِهٖ وَسَلَّم set out from Madinah on the last Thursday of *Zul-Qa'dah* and reached Zul-Hulayfah, which is the *Meeqat* of the people of Madinah, where he صَلَّى اللهُ عَلَيْهِ وَاٰلِهٖ وَسَلَّم donned the Ihram, and then entered Makkah on 4th of *Zul-Hijjah*.

He صَلَّى اللهُ عَلَيْهِ وَاٰلِهٖ وَسَلَّم performed *Tawaf*, offered *Nafl* at *Maqaam Ibrahim* and performed *Sa'i* of Safa and Marwah. Then, on the 8th of *Zul-Hijjah*, he صَلَّى اللهُ عَلَيْهِ وَاٰلِهٖ وَسَلَّم went to Mina and on the 9th, he صَلَّى اللهُ عَلَيْهِ وَاٰلِهٖ وَسَلَّم went to 'Arafat, where he صَلَّى اللهُ عَلَيْهِ وَاٰلِهٖ وَسَلَّم stayed in a tent. When the sun passed the meridian, he صَلَّى اللهُ عَلَيْهِ وَاٰلِهٖ وَسَلَّم mounted his she-camel, 'Qaswa', and delivered the sermon.

In this sermon, he صَلَّى اللّٰهُ عَلَيْهِ وَاٰلِهٖ وَسَلَّم announced many necessary commandants and also announced the abrogation of all the evils and taboo customs of the era of ignorance.

Farewell Sermon

Below are a few points from the last sermon:

- Your Lord is One and undoubtedly your father (Sayyiduna Adam عَلَيْهِ السَّلَام) is one. No Arab has any superiority over any non-Arab and no non-Arab has any superiority over any Arab; no white has any superiority over any black and no black has any superiority over any white, but by piety.
- All humans are the offspring of Adam, and Adam was made from clay. Now, all the claims of excellence and superiority, all the demands of blood and money, and all revenges are under my feet.
- O people! Every Muslim is the brother of another Muslim and all the Muslims are brothers of one another.
- It is not permissible for anyone that he takes anything from his brother, except for the thing for which his brother agrees and gives happily. O people! Do not inflict cruelty on yourselves and on others.
- Your life and your wealth are as *Haraam* for each other until the Judgement Day as this day, this month, and this city of yours is sacred for you.
- O people! Treat women well!
- The Beloved Prophet صَلَّى اللّٰهُ عَلَيْهِ وَاٰلِهٖ وَسَلَّم then said: "When Allah Almighty will ask you about me, what will you say?" Blessed companions humbly said: "You have conveyed the message of Allah and fulfilled the right of Prophethood." The Final Messenger of Allah صَلَّى اللّٰهُ عَلَيْهِ وَاٰلِهٖ وَسَلَّم raised his blessed finger towards the sky and said three times: "O Allah! Be my witness."

After this, he صَلَّى اللّٰهُ عَلَيْهِ وَاٰلِهٖ وَسَلَّم was given the confirmation of the completion of the religion through Divine revelation and then he صَلَّى اللّٰهُ عَلَيْهِ وَاٰلِهٖ وَسَلَّم completed his Hajj.

Phenomenal Impact of the Farewell Sermon

The Final Messenger of Allah صَلَّى اللّٰهُ عَلَيْهِ وَاٰلِهٖ وَسَلَّم delivered this sermon approximately fourteen and a half centuries ago. It is astonishing that while he صَلَّى اللّٰهُ عَلَيْهِ وَاٰلِهٖ وَسَلَّم was delivering this sermon, he صَلَّى اللّٰهُ عَلَيْهِ وَاٰلِهٖ وَسَلَّم was sitting on the saddle of a she-camel. It was the glory of his excellent simplicity.

This sermon is a golden and bright chapter in human history. This sermon contains unprecedented guidance about human rights, especially the rights of women, the rights of slaves, protection of life, possessions and honour, economic reforms, rulings on inheritance, commandments on debt and debtors, as well as guidance on politics and religion. This sermon is the essence of all Islamic teachings and an international manifesto of rights and duties. This sermon is regarded as a constitution and an evergreen message even today for Muslims. This sermon is as important today as it was fourteen and a half centuries ago. This sermon contains the guidance which humanity needs and the lessons which, if implemented by people, will lead mankind to great heights.

Distribution of BLESSED HAIR

As well as in Arafat, the Beloved Prophet صَلَّى اللّٰهُ عَلَيْهِ وَاٰلِهٖ وَسَلَّم also delivered a sermon in Mina, in which, he صَلَّى اللّٰهُ عَلَيْهِ وَاٰلِهٖ وَسَلَّم mentioned many rulings and commandments like he did in the sermon of Arafat. He صَلَّى اللّٰهُ عَلَيْهِ وَاٰلِهٖ وَسَلَّم then went to the slaughterhouse, where out of one hundred camels, he صَلَّى اللّٰهُ عَلَيْهِ وَاٰلِهٖ وَسَلَّم slaughtered some camels with his blessed hands, and then ordered Sayyiduna Ali رَضِىَ اللّٰهُ عَنْهُ to slaughter the remaining ones. After the animal sacrifice, he صَلَّى اللّٰهُ عَلَيْهِ وَاٰلِهٖ وَسَلَّم had his blessed head shaved. He صَلَّى اللّٰهُ عَلَيْهِ وَاٰلِهٖ وَسَلَّم then gave some of this hair to Sayyiduna Abu Talhah Ansari رَضِىَ اللّٰهُ عَنْهُ and ordered him to distribute the remaining hair amongst the Muslims. He صَلَّى اللّٰهُ عَلَيْهِ وَاٰلِهٖ وَسَلَّم then went to the Zamzam Well and drank Zamzam, and then after performing the farewell Tawaf, returned to Madinah with *Muhajireen* and *Ansar*.

Final Illness and Blessed Passing

In the 11th year of migration, on the 20th or 22nd Safar, the Final Messenger of Allah صَلَّى اللهُ عَلَيْهِ وَاٰلِهٖ وَسَلَّم went to *Jannat-ul-Baqi* at midnight. When he صَلَّى اللهُ عَلَيْهِ وَاٰلِهٖ وَسَلَّم returned from there, he صَلَّى اللهُ عَلَيْهِ وَاٰلِهٖ وَسَلَّم started feeling unwell. His health further deteriorated in the next few days.

With the permission of all of his blessed wives, he صَلَّى اللهُ عَلَيْهِ وَاٰلِهٖ وَسَلَّم stayed in the blessed room of Sayyidatuna 'Aisha. When he صَلَّى اللهُ عَلَيْهِ وَاٰلِهٖ وَسَلَّم felt very weak, he صَلَّى اللهُ عَلَيْهِ وَاٰلِهٖ وَسَلَّم ordered for Sayyiduna Abu Bakr رَضِیَ اللهُ عَنْهُ to lead *Salah* on his prayer mat. Sayyiduna Abu Bakr رَضِیَ اللهُ عَنْهُ led seventeen *Salahs* during this time.

A little while before the blessed passing, Sayyiduna Abdul Rahman bin Abu Bakr رَضِیَ اللهُ عَنْهُ, the brother of Sayyidatuna 'Aisha رَضِیَ اللهُ عَنْهَا, came with a fresh *Miswak* in his hand. The Beloved Prophet صَلَّى اللهُ عَلَيْهِ وَاٰلِهٖ وَسَلَّم looked at him, his blessed gaze fixated. Sayyidatuna 'Aisha رَضِیَ اللهُ عَنْهَا understood that he صَلَّى اللهُ عَلَيْهِ وَاٰلِهٖ وَسَلَّم wished for the *Miswak*. She immediately took the *Miswak*, made it soft with her teeth and placed it in his blessed hand, after which, he صَلَّى اللهُ عَلَيْهِ وَاٰلِهٖ وَسَلَّم performed *Miswak*.

The Beloved Prophet صَلَّى اللهُ عَلَيْهِ وَاٰلِهٖ وَسَلَّم veiled from this world on Monday in *Rabi' al-Awwal*. According to the famous opinion, it was the 12th *Rabi al-Awwal* in the 11th year of migration.

His blessed passing gave the blessed companions a great shock. According to the will of the Beloved Prophet صَلَّى اللهُ عَلَيْهِ وَاٰلِهٖ وَسَلَّم, his funeral rites were performed by his *Ahl al-Bayt* and his family members. His blessed Janazah remained in the blessed room of Sayyidatuna 'Aisha رَضِیَ اللهُ عَنْهَا. Sayyiduna Abbas رَضِیَ اللهُ عَنْهُ gave the following details of how the funeral *Salah* of the Beloved Prophet صَلَّى اللهُ عَلَيْهِ وَاٰلِهٖ وَسَلَّم was offered:

When the Final Messenger of Allah صَلَّى اللهُ عَلَيْهِ وَاٰلِهٖ وَسَلَّم passed away, the men first entered and they recited *Salat* and *Salaam* individually without any Imam. Then, the women entered and they also recited *Salat* and *Salaam* upon him. Then, the children entered and they also did the same. Then, the slaves went and they also recited *Salat* and *Salaam* upon him. No one did *Imamah* (led a prayer) over him.

In the beginning, there was a difference of opinion amongst blessed companions as to where the Beloved Prophet صَلَّى اللهُ عَلَيْهِ وَاٰلِهٖ وَسَلَّم would be buried. On this occasion, Sayyiduna Abu Bakr Siddeeq رَضِیَ اللهُ عَنْهُ said: "I have heard from the Beloved Prophet صَلَّى اللهُ عَلَيْهِ وَاٰلِهٖ وَسَلَّم that after the passing of every prophet, he is buried where he has passed away." After listening to this blessed Hadith, people prepared the grave of the Beloved Prophet صَلَّى اللهُ عَلَيْهِ وَاٰلِهٖ وَسَلَّم at that very place (blessed room of Sayyidah 'Aisha) and he صَلَّى اللهُ عَلَيْهِ وَاٰلِهٖ وَسَلَّم was buried there. Sayyiduna Abu Talhah Ansari رَضِیَ اللهُ عَنْهُ prepared grave with a niche in the wall; Sayyiduna Ali, Sayyiduna Fadl Bin Abbas, Sayyiduna Quthum Bin Abbas and Sayyiduna Abbas رَضِیَ اللهُ عَنْهُم lowered the blessed body in the luminous grave.

Chapter 11

Blessed Attributes and Appearance of the Holy Prophet ﷺ

Blessed Appearance

Sayyiduna Anas رَضِیَ اللّٰہُ عَنْہُ has said: "The blessed body of the Final Messenger of Allah صَلَّی اللّٰہُ عَلَیۡہِ وَاٰلِہٖ وَسَلَّم was very soft and delicate. I have never even seen silk softer and more delicate than his blessed body. I have never smelt any other fragrance better than the fragrance of his blessed body.[1]

It was one of the unique attributes of the Beloved Prophet صَلَّی اللّٰہُ عَلَیۡہِ وَاٰلِہٖ وَسَلَّم that he had no shadow. His shadow did not appear on the ground in the sunlight, in the moonlight or in any other light.[2]

Between both of his shoulders was the Seal of Prophethood that was equal to the size of a pigeon egg. He صَلَّی اللّٰہُ عَلَیۡہِ وَاٰلِہٖ وَسَلَّم was of a medium height. It was his miracle that when he صَلَّی اللّٰہُ عَلَیۡہِ وَاٰلِہٖ وَسَلَّم would separate from people, he صَلَّی اللّٰہُ عَلَیۡہِ وَاٰلِہٖ وَسَلَّم would appear medium-tall in height and when he صَلَّی اللّٰہُ عَلَیۡہِ وَاٰلِہٖ وَسَلَّم would sit or walk with others, he صَلَّی اللّٰہُ عَلَیۡہِ وَاٰلِہٖ وَسَلَّم would look the tallest of all.

His blessed head was large; his blessed hair was slightly curly; his blessed face was the reflection of Divine beauty and shone like the moon of the fourteenth night of the lunar month. [3]

Sayyiduna Anas رَضِیَ اللّٰہُ عَنْہُ has further added: "The colour of the blessed face of the Beloved Prophet صَلَّی اللّٰہُ عَلَیۡہِ وَاٰلِہٖ وَسَلَّم was neither absolutely white like chalk, nor was it wheatish, but rather, his blessed face was red and white and glowing." [4]

His blessed eyebrows were extended and thin, and looked as if they were joined to each other from a distance. There was a vein between them which would stand out in times of anger. His luminous eyes were big and naturally appeared as though kohl had been applied in them. [5]

---

1 Bukhari, Kitab, al-Munaqib, vol. 2, p. 489, Hadith 3561
2 Sharah al Zurqani Ali Al-Al-Mawahib, vol. 5, pp. 524-525
3 Sharah al Zurqani Ali Al-Al-Mawahib, vol. 5, p. 485
4 Al-Shumai'l al-Muhammadiyah, p. 15
5 Al Shuma'il al-Muhammadiyah, pp. 19-21

It was the miracle of his luminous eyes that just as he صَلَّى اللّٰهُ عَلَيْهِ وَاٰلِهٖ وَسَلَّم would see the things in front of him, he صَلَّى اللّٰهُ عَلَيْهِ وَاٰلِهٖ وَسَلَّم would also see the things that were behind him.

Like his luminous eyes, his blessed ears also had miraculous glory. He صَلَّى اللّٰهُ عَلَيْهِ وَاٰلِهٖ وَسَلَّم has himself said: "I see those things which no one amongst you sees, and I hear the sounds which no one amongst you hears." [1]

His blessed forehead was bright and broad. His blessed cheeks were soft, delicate and smooth. His blessed teeth were wide and sparkling. When he صَلَّى اللّٰهُ عَلَيْهِ وَاٰلِهٖ وَسَلَّم would converse, light would emanate from between his front two teeth. When he صَلَّى اللّٰهُ عَلَيْهِ وَاٰلِهٖ وَسَلَّم would smile in the dark, light would spread everywhere. [2]

His blessed tongue was the channel of Divine revelation and was extremely eloquent. When excellent eloquent speakers listened to his speech, they would be stunned. His blessed voice was very beautiful; its excellence is that during the sermons, all people, whether near or at a distance, would listen to his sacred speech equally well wherever they were seated. [3]

His blessed hands were very soft, delicate and fleshy. The person with whom he صَلَّى اللّٰهُ عَلَيْهِ وَاٰلِهٖ وَسَلَّم would shake hands would be left with fragrant hands for the entire day.

His blessed feet were wide and fleshy. They were so soft and delicate that water did not stay on them. While walking, he صَلَّى اللّٰهُ عَلَيْهِ وَاٰلِهٖ وَسَلَّم would put his steps on the ground[4] in a dignified manner. When he صَلَّى اللّٰهُ عَلَيْهِ وَاٰلِهٖ وَسَلَّم would walk, it seemed as if he was descending from a height. He صَلَّى اللّٰهُ عَلَيْهِ وَاٰلِهٖ وَسَلَّم would take every step firmly. [5]

---

1 Al Khasais al-Kubra Laswati, vol. 1, p. 104
2 Al-Shuma'il Al-Muhammadiyah, pp. 21,26
3 Sharah al-Zurqani Al-al-Muwahib, vol. 5, pp. 444, 445
4 Al Shuma'il al-Muhammadiyah, p. 21
5 Al-Shuma'il Al-Muhammadiyah, p. 86

Favourite foods

The blessed life of the Beloved Prophet صَلَّى اللهُ عَلَيْهِ وَاٰلِهٖ وَسَلَّم was a complete model of simplicity and piety. He صَلَّى اللهُ عَلَيْهِ وَاٰلِهٖ وَسَلَّم, therefore, never paid attention to delicious foods. He صَلَّى اللهُ عَلَيْهِ وَاٰلِهٖ وَسَلَّم even did not eat chapati even once in his life. Despite this, he صَلَّى اللهُ عَلَيْهِ وَاٰلِهٖ وَسَلَّم was refined regarding his food.

In Arabia, there is a dish called 'Hays' which is prepared by mixing ghee, cheese and dates. He صَلَّى اللهُ عَلَيْهِ وَاٰلِهٖ وَسَلَّم had an inclination towards this food.[1]

He صَلَّى اللهُ عَلَيْهِ وَاٰلِهٖ وَسَلَّم particularly liked meat, vinegar, honey, olive oil and gourd. He صَلَّى اللهُ عَلَيْهِ وَاٰلِهٖ وَسَلَّم would also eat dates and barley flour quite often. He صَلَّى اللهُ عَلَيْهِ وَاٰلِهٖ وَسَلَّم liked cold fresh water very much. At times, he صَلَّى اللهُ عَلَيْهِ وَاٰلِهٖ وَسَلَّم would drink pure milk and sometimes would drink water-mixed milk. Whatever he صَلَّى اللهُ عَلَيْهِ وَاٰلِهٖ وَسَلَّم would drink, he صَلَّى اللهُ عَلَيْهِ وَاٰلِهٖ وَسَلَّم would drink in three sips.

Favourite clothing

Mostly, the Final Messenger of Allah صَلَّى اللهُ عَلَيْهِ وَاٰلِهٖ وَسَلَّم would wear cotton clothes. He صَلَّى اللهُ عَلَيْهِ وَاٰلِهٖ وَسَلَّم did not adhere to wearing a particular type of outfit continuously. The gown (Jubbah)[2], Qaba[3], loose long shirt, sarong, Hullah, shawl, Imamah (turban), cap, and leather socks all have attained the privilege of being worn by him. In colours, he صَلَّى اللهُ عَلَيْهِ وَاٰلِهٖ وَسَلَّم liked white the most. According to another narration, he صَلَّى اللهُ عَلَيْهِ وَاٰلِهٖ وَسَلَّم liked green a lot as well.

---

1 Sunan Kubra Lil-Nasai, vol. 2, p. 114, Hadith 2631

2 A type of loose coat whose sleeves reach the forearm and whose overall length is from the chest to the feet. It is generally worn by Islamic scholars.

3 A type of coat which is open from the front and is worn over the clothes.

Blessed riding animals

The Beloved Prophet صَلَّى اللهُ عَلَيْهِ وَاٰلِهٖ وَسَلَّم would like horse riding very much. Besides horses, he صَلَّى اللهُ عَلَيْهِ وَاٰلِهٖ وَسَلَّم also rode on camels, mules and donkeys.

Blessed habits and manners

The Beloved Prophet صَلَّى اللهُ عَلَيْهِ وَاٰلِهٖ وَسَلَّم was outstanding not only in his blessed appearance, but also in his blessed character. He صَلَّى اللهُ عَلَيْهِ وَاٰلِهٖ وَسَلَّم would help the weak. He صَلَّى اللهُ عَلَيْهِ وَاٰلِهٖ وَسَلَّم would not only be soft-hearted to his own people, but even to his enemies. He صَلَّى اللهُ عَلَيْهِ وَاٰلِهٖ وَسَلَّم was humble, and would not get angry nor take revenge for his own personal sake. He صَلَّى اللهُ عَلَيْهِ وَاٰلِهٖ وَسَلَّم would visit the sick and comfort sad people. He صَلَّى اللهُ عَلَيْهِ وَاٰلِهٖ وَسَلَّم would treat people equally, whether they were rich or poor. He صَلَّى اللهُ عَلَيْهِ وَاٰلِهٖ وَسَلَّم would accept the invitation of all.

He صَلَّى اللهُ عَلَيْهِ وَاٰلِهٖ وَسَلَّم liked to do his work with his own hands. He صَلَّى اللهُ عَلَيْهِ وَاٰلِهٖ وَسَلَّم was the most just and most chaste in the entire universe. He صَلَّى اللهُ عَلَيْهِ وَاٰلِهٖ وَسَلَّم would converse in a clear and dignified manner. There was so much fluency and beauty in his speech that if someone wanted to count the sentences, he could.

He صَلَّى اللهُ عَلَيْهِ وَاٰلِهٖ وَسَلَّم was very modest. Even his enemies would praise his trustworthiness and truthfulness. His manners were so excellent that Allah Almighty has Himself said:

وَ اِنَّكَ لَعَلٰى خُلُقٍ عَظِيْمٍ ۝

And (O Beloved), your (excellent) character is undoubtedly of a superb standard.[1]

---

1 *[Kanz-ul-Iman (translation of Quran)] (Part 29, Surah Al-Qalam, Verse 4)*

Virtues and Attributes

The Final Messenger of Allah صَلَّى اللّٰهُ عَلَيْهِ وَاٰلِهٖ وَسَلَّم holds the highest rank amongst all the prophets. His countless virtues and attributes have been mentioned in the Holy Quran and blessed Hadith. Let's read some of them:

- Other blessed prophets were sent to a specific nation, but the Beloved Prophet صَلَّى اللّٰهُ عَلَيْهِ وَاٰلِهٖ وَسَلَّم was sent to all humans and *jinns*, and in fact all angels, animals and non-living things.
- As it is mandatory for humans to obey the Beloved Prophet صَلَّى اللّٰهُ عَلَيْهِ وَاٰلِهٖ وَسَلَّم, similarly, it is necessary for all of the creation to obey him.
- He صَلَّى اللّٰهُ عَلَيْهِ وَاٰلِهٖ وَسَلَّم is a mercy for angels, humans, *jinns*, *hoors*, animals and non-living things; in short for all. He صَلَّى اللّٰهُ عَلَيْهِ وَاٰلِهٖ وَسَلَّم is especially merciful to the Muslims.
- He صَلَّى اللّٰهُ عَلَيْهِ وَاٰلِهٖ وَسَلَّم is *Khatam al-Nabiyyeen*, i.e. Allah Almighty has ended Prophethood with his arrival. No prophet could come in his age or can come after him. The one who believes or considers it possible that Prophethood could to be given to someone during his blessed age or can be given to someone after his passing is a disbeliever.
- The Beloved Prophet صَلَّى اللّٰهُ عَلَيْهِ وَاٰلِهٖ وَسَلَّم is the best and most superior of all creation. The attributes which were bestowed upon other prophets one by one have been gathered in him. In addition, he has also been blessed with the attributes which no other prophet could have, but rather whatever others had, they had for his sake, or rather, through his hands.
- One of his unique virtues is *Mi'raaj*. When he صَلَّى اللّٰهُ عَلَيْهِ وَاٰلِهٖ وَسَلَّم went to *Masjid al-Aqsa* from *Masjid al- Haraam* and from there to all seven skies and to the *Kursi* and the *Arsh*, and in fact beyond the *Arsh* in a short part of the night physically, there, he صَلَّى اللّٰهُ عَلَيْهِ وَاٰلِهٖ وَسَلَّم attained the special closeness that no human or angel has ever attained or will ever attain. He

صَلَّى اللّٰهُ عَلَيْهِ وَاٰلِهٖ وَسَلَّم beheld the Divine beauty, heard the Divine speech directly and saw every particle of the sky and the earth with his blessed eyes.

- Love for him is the centre of *Iman* (faith); in fact, the true meaning of Iman is to have love for him. As long as a person does not love him more than his mother, father, children and the entire world, he cannot be a true Muslim.

- Obedience to him is in fact obedience to Allah Almighty; in fact, obedience to Allah Almighty is impossible without obedience to him. Even if a person is offering obligatory *Salah* and he صَلَّى اللّٰهُ عَلَيْهِ وَاٰلِهٖ وَسَلَّم calls him, that person should immediately reply and go to him. No matter how long this person converses with him, he is continuously in *Salah*. It does not intervene in the *Salah*.

- Just as the reverence and respect for the Beloved Prophet صَلَّى اللّٰهُ عَلَيْهِ وَاٰلِهٖ وَسَلَّم was the greatest obligatory act when he was in front of the physical eyes of people in world, it is still the greatest obligatory act now as well. When he is mentioned, one should listen to it with humility of the body and presence of the heart, and it is *Wajib* to recite *Salat* as soon as one hears his blessed name. [1]

- Allah Almighty bestowed countless miracles upon him. His miracles include splitting the moon in two pieces, making the sun rise again after it had set, making pieces of wood shine like a bulb, making the water of brackish wells sweet with his blessed saliva, assisting people from huge distances away, making springs gush out from his fingers, making rain fall by his gesture, conversing with trees and stones, making a little food and milk sufficient for a large number of people, trees moving and coming to say *Salam* to him, and animals speaking to him like humans. The Holy Quran is also one of his miracles.

---

1 Bahar-e-Shari›at, vol. 1, p. 76, Part 1

QURANIC VERSES AND THE GLORY OF THE PROPHET صَلَّى اللهُ عَلَيْهِ وَسَلَّم

One of the most important aspects of the virtues of the Final Messenger of Allah صَلَّى اللهُ عَلَيْهِ وَاٰلِهٖ وَسَلَّم is that Allah Almighty has Himself mentioned His dignity and glory in the Holy Quran at many places. A few such verses have been mentioned below:

Command to seek forgiveness for sins after appearing before the Beloved Prophet صَلَّى اللهُ عَلَيْهِ وَسَلَّم

وَلَوْ اَنَّهُمْ اِذْ ظَّلَمُوْۤا اَنْفُسَهُمْ جَآءُوْكَ فَاسْتَغْفَرُوا اللّٰهَ وَ اسْتَغْفَرَ لَهُمُ الرَّسُوْلُ

لَوَجَدُوا اللّٰهَ تَوَّابًا رَّحِيْمًا ﴿۶۴﴾

And if when they do injustice to their own souls (by committing sins), O Beloved, they should then present themselves in your august court, and then seek forgiveness from Allah, and the

Messenger intercedes for them; so they would definitely find Allah the Greatest Acceptor of repentance, the Most Merciful.[1]

Good News of the Arrival of Mustafa and Command to Believe in him

يٰۤاَيُّهَا النَّاسُ قَدْ جَآءَكُمُ الرَّسُوْلُ بِالْحَقِّ مِنْ رَّبِّكُمْ فَاٰمِنُوْا خَيْرًا لَّكُمْ ؕ

O people! This Messenger has come to you with the truth from your Lord; so, accept faith for your own good.[2]

Expressing the Glory and Dignity of the Beloved Prophet ﷺ

يٰۤاَهْلَ الْكِتٰبِ قَدْ جَآءَكُمْ رَسُوْلُنَا يُبَيِّنُ لَكُمْ كَثِيْرًا مِّمَّا كُنْتُمْ تُخْفُوْنَ مِنَ
الْكِتٰبِ وَ يَعْفُوْا عَنْ كَثِيْرٍ ؕ۬ قَدْ جَآءَكُمْ مِّنَ اللّٰهِ نُوْرٌ وَّ كِتٰبٌ مُّبِيْنٌ ﴿۱۵﴾

O People of the Book! Indeed, there has come to you this Messenger of Ours (i.e. the Prophet Muhammad); that he reveals to you many things which you had concealed in the Book, and forgives several of them (by not mentioning the things you had concealed). Indeed, towards you has come a light from Allah (i.e. the Prophet Muhammad), and a Clear Book (i.e. the Holy Qur'aan).[3]

The Attributes of the Beloved Prophet ﷺ and his Affection towards the Ummah

لَقَدْ جَآءَكُمْ رَسُوْلٌ مِّنْ اَنْفُسِكُمْ عَزِيْزٌ عَلَيْهِ مَا عَنِتُّمْ حَرِيْصٌ عَلَيْكُمْ
بِالْمُؤْمِنِيْنَ رَءُوْفٌ رَّحِيْمٌ ﴿۱۲۸﴾

1 *[Kanz-ul-Iman (translation of Quran)] (Part 5, Surah Al-Nisa, Verse 64)*
2 *[Kanz-ul-Iman (translation of Quran)] (Part 170, Surah Al-Nisa, Verse 170)*
3 *[Kanz-ul-Iman (translation of Quran)] (Part 6, Surah Al-Maa'idah, Verse 15)*

Indeed, there has come to you that Messenger from amongst yourselves; heavy upon him is your suffering, he immensely desires your well-being; utmost kind, merciful for the Muslims.[1]

Event of the Mi'raaj of the Beloved Prophet ﷺ from Masjid al-Haraam to Masjid al-Aqsa

سُبْحٰنَ الَّذِیْۤ اَسْرٰى بِعَبْدِهٖ لَیْلًا مِّنَ الْمَسْجِدِ الْحَرَامِ اِلَى الْمَسْجِدِ الْاَقْصَا الَّذِیْ
بٰرَكْنَا حَوْلَهٗ لِنُرِیَهٗ مِنْ اٰیٰتِنَاؕ اِنَّهٗ هُوَ السَّمِیْعُ الْبَصِیْرُ (۱)

Glory be to Him Who took His bondsman by the night from the Sacred Mosque (the Ka'bah) to Al-Aqsa Mosque around which We have placed blessing, in order that We may show him Our great Signs. Indeed, He is the All-Hearing, the All-Seeing.[2]

The Mercy of the Beloved Prophet ﷺ

وَ مَاۤ اَرْسَلْنٰكَ اِلَّا رَحْمَةً لِّلْعٰلَمِیْنَ (۱۰۷)

And We did not send you (O Beloved) but as a mercy for all the worlds.[3]

The Universal Prophethood of the Beloved Prophet ﷺ

وَ مَاۤ اَرْسَلْنٰكَ اِلَّا كَآفَّةً لِّلنَّاسِ بَشِیْرًا وَّ نَذِیْرًا وَّ لٰكِنَّ اَكْثَرَ النَّاسِ لَا
یَعْلَمُوْنَ (۲۸)

And O Beloved Prophet, We have not sent you except with such Prophethood that encompasses the entire mankind, as a conveyor of glad tidings and warning, but most people know not.[4]

---

1 *[Kanz-ul-Iman (translation of Quran)] (Part 11, Surah Al-Tawbah, Verse 128)*
2 *[Kanz-ul-Iman (translation of Quran)] (Part 15, Surah Bani Israel, Verse 1)*
3 *[Kanz-ul-Iman (translation of Quran)] (Part 17, Surah Ambiya, Verse 107)*
4 *[Kanz-ul-Iman (translation of Quran)] (Part 22, Surah Saba, Verse 28)*

Allah Almighty and the Angels Sending Salat upon the Beloved Prophet ﷺ, and Command for Muslims to Send Salat and Salam

إِنَّ اللّٰهَ وَمَلٰٓئِكَتَهٗ يُصَلُّوْنَ عَلَى النَّبِيِّ ؕ يٰٓاَيُّهَا الَّذِيْنَ اٰمَنُوْا صَلُّوْا عَلَيْهِ وَ
سَلِّمُوْا تَسْلِيْمًا ﴿۵۶﴾

Indeed, Allah and His angels send blessings on the Conveyor of the unseen news (i.e. the Prophet). O believers! (You too) send blessings and abundant salutations upon him.[1]

The Glory and Dignity of the Beloved Prophet ﷺ

وَالنَّجْمِ اِذَا هَوٰى ۙ﴿۱﴾ مَا ضَلَّ صَاحِبُكُمْ وَمَا غَوٰى ۚ﴿۲﴾ وَمَا يَنْطِقُ عَنِ
الْهَوٰى ؕ﴿۳﴾ اِنْ هُوَ اِلَّا وَحْیٌ يُّوْحٰى ۙ﴿۴﴾

By the oath of that beloved shining star Muhammad, when he descended from Mi'raaj (i.e. the Ascension). Your companion (i.e. the Prophet Muhammad) has not strayed, nor was he misled. And he does not say anything of his own desire. It is not but revelation which is sent down upon him.[2]

Expression of the Beloved Prophet's glory through oaths

وَالضُّحٰى ۙ﴿۱﴾ وَالَّيْلِ اِذَا سَجٰى ۙ﴿۲﴾ مَا وَدَّعَكَ رَبُّكَ وَمَا قَلٰى ؕ﴿۳﴾ وَلَلْاٰخِرَةُ خَيْرٌ لَّكَ
مِنَ الْاُوْلٰى ؕ﴿۴﴾ وَلَسَوْفَ يُعْطِيْكَ رَبُّكَ فَتَرْضٰى ؕ﴿۵﴾

By the oath of the forenoon. And by the night when it covers (everything with its darkness). That your Lord has neither abandoned you (O Beloved), nor did He dislike you. And indeed,

1 *[Kanz-ul-Iman (translation of Quran)] (Part 22, Surah Al-Ahzaab, Verse 56)*
2 *[Kanz-ul-Iman (translation of Quran)] (Part 27, Surah Al-Najm, Verse 1-4)*

the latter is better for you than the former. And indeed, it is close that your Lord will give you so much that you will be pleased.[1]

The Divine Gifts Given to the Beloved Prophet ﷺ

وَرَفَعْنَا لَكَ ذِكْرَكَ ﴿٤﴾

And We have elevated your remembrance for your sake.[2]

The Bestowal of Countless Qualities upon him

إِنَّآ أَعْطَيْنٰكَ الْكَوْثَرَ ﴿١﴾

O Beloved, We have indeed bestowed upon you countless excellences.[3]

Glory of Mustafa in the Light of Blessed Hadith

In blessed Hadith, the Final Messenger of Allah ﷺ has also mentioned his own excellence at many places. A few such Hadith are mentioned below.

Chief of All the Offspring of Adam

The Final Messenger of Allah صَلَّى اللهُ عَلَيْهِ وَاٰلِهٖ وَسَلَّم has said:

أَنَا سَيِّدُ وَلَدِ آدَمَ يَوْمَ الْقِيَامَةِ وَلَا فَخْرَ وَبِيَدِي لِوَاءُ الْحَمْدِ وَلَا فَخْرَ وَمَا مِنْ نَبِيٍّ يَوْمَئِذٍ آدَمُ فَمَنْ سِوَاهُ إِلَّا تَحْتَ لِوَائِي

On Judgement Day, I will be the chief of all humankind and I am not proud of it. In my hand will be the flag of *Liwa al-Hamd*, and I am not proud of it. On Judgement Day, (Sayyiduna) Adam, as

1 *[Kanz-ul-Iman (translation of Quran)] (Part 30, Surah Al-Duha, Verse 1-5)*
2 *[Kanz-ul-Iman (translation of Quran)] (Part 30, Surah Alam Nashrah, Verse 4)*
3 *[Kanz-ul-Iman (translation of Quran)] (Part 30, Surah Al-Kawthar, Verse 1)*

well as all, will be under my flag.

Five Attributes of Mustafa

The Final Messenger of Allah صَلَّى اللّٰهُ عَلَيْهِ وَاٰلِهٖ وَسَلَّم has said: "Five such things have been bestowed upon me which were not given to anyone else before me. (1) I was helped through the awe of the distance of one month. (2) Spoils of war have been made *Halal* for me, though they were not *Halal* for anyone before me. (3) The entire earth has been made the place of *Sajdah* for me, and soil has been made pure for me. So, if *Salah* time begins for any of my followers, he should offer *Salah* wherever he is. (4) The station of intercession has been bestowed upon me. (5) Every prophet was sent to a specific nation, whereas, I have been sent to all people.'

First Amongst Prophets

Sayyiduna Abu Hurayrah رَضِیَ اللّٰهُ عَنْهُ has said that once, the blessed companions رَضِیَ اللّٰهُ عَنْهُم humbly said to the Beloved Prophet صَلَّى اللّٰهُ عَلَيْهِ وَاٰلِهٖ وَسَلَّم: "O Prophet of Allah صَلَّى اللّٰهُ عَلَيْهِ وَاٰلِهٖ وَسَلَّم! Please tell us, when were you blessed with Prophethood?" He صَلَّى اللّٰهُ عَلَيْهِ وَاٰلِهٖ وَسَلَّم replied: "I was even a Prophet at the time when the creation of Adam was in the stage between body and soul."

Glory of Mustafa in the Words of Umar

Once, Sayyiduna Umar رَضِیَ اللّٰهُ عَنْهُ mentioned the glory of the Final Messenger of Allah صَلَّى اللّٰهُ عَلَيْهِ وَاٰلِهٖ وَسَلَّم, with tears flowing from his eyes. Please read a few extracts of his beautiful speech:

O Prophet of Allah صَلَّى اللّٰهُ عَلَيْهِ وَاٰلِهٖ وَسَلَّم! May my mother and father be sacrificed for you! In the beginning, you would deliver the sermon on the trunk of a date tree, then due to a large number of people, you started delivering the sermon from the pulpit. That trunk of a date tree kept weeping because of the separation from you until you placed your affectionate hand on it, and then it gained peace. Due to the separation from you, your *Ummah* deserve to weep more.

O Prophet of Allah صَلَّى اللهُ عَلَيْهِ وَاٰلِهٖ وَسَلَّم! May my mother and father be sacrificed for you! Your status is so high before your Lord that He has declared that obedience to you is obedience to Him.

مَنْ يُّطِعِ الرَّسُوْلَ فَقَدْ اَطَاعَ اللّٰهَ ۚ

Whosoever has obeyed the Messenger, he has indeed obeyed Allah,[1]

O Prophet of Allah صَلَّى اللهُ عَلَيْهِ وَاٰلِهٖ وَسَلَّم! May my mother and father be sacrificed for you! Your status is so high before your Lord that He sent you after all prophets, but mentioned you before all prophets. It has been stated:

وَاِذْ اَخَذْنَا مِنَ النَّبِيّٖنَ مِيْثَاقَهُمْ وَمِنْكَ وَمِنْ نُّوْحٍ وَّاِبْرٰهِيْمَ وَمُوْسٰى وَعِيْسَى
ابْنِ مَرْيَمَ ۪ وَاَخَذْنَا مِنْهُمْ مِّيْثَاقًا غَلِيْظًا ۙ﴿۷﴾

And, O Beloved, remember when We took a covenant from the Prophets, and from you, and from Nooh, and Ibrahim, and Moosa, and 'Eisa; the son of Maryam; and We took a solemn covenant from them.[2]

O Prophet of Allah صَلَّى اللهُ عَلَيْهِ وَاٰلِهٖ وَسَلَّم! May my mother and father be sacrificed for you! Allah Almighty gave the miracle to Sayyiduna Musa عَلَيْهِ السَّلَام that springs gushed out from stones (when he struck them with his staff), but even more amazing are the springs that gushed out from your blessed fingers.

O Prophet of Allah صَلَّى اللهُ عَلَيْهِ وَاٰلِهٖ وَسَلَّم! May my mother and father be sacrificed for you! Allah Almighty gave Sayyiduna Sulayman عَلَيْهِ السَّلَام such control over the wind that its blowing in the morning and its blowing in the evening were equal to the travel of one month, but

---

1 *[Kanz-ul-Iman (translation of Quran)] (Part 5, Surah Al-Nisa, Verse 80)*
2 *[Kanz-ul-Iman (translation of Quran)] (Part 21, Surah Al-Ahzaab, Verse 7)*

your riding animal *Buraaq* is more astonishing than that on which you visited all seven skies and on the same night, you also offered *Fajr Salah* after coming back to Makkah.

O Prophet of Allah صَلَّى اللهُ عَلَيْهِ وَاٰلِهٖ وَسَلَّم! May my mother and father be sacrificed for you! Allah Almighty bestowed Sayyiduna Isa عَلَيْهِ السَّلَام with the miracle of raising the dead, but even more amazing is that poisonous meat of roasted mutton talking to you and saying: "Do not eat me because poison has been mixed in me."

O Prophet of Allah صَلَّى اللهُ عَلَيْهِ وَاٰلِهٖ وَسَلَّم! May my mother and father be sacrificed for you! Sayyiduna Nuh عَلَيْهِ السَّلَام made Du'a for the destruction of his nation, and said:

رَّبِّ لَا تَذَرْ عَلَى الْاَرْضِ مِنَ الْكٰفِرِيْنَ دَيَّارًا ﴿۲۶﴾

And requested Nooh, 'O my Lord, do not leave any of the disbelievers residing on the earth.'[1]

If you had made Du'a in the same way, we would have been destroyed, but it is your affection towards us that you were tormented, hurt, and wounded, but even then, you said nothing except for goodness. Whenever your nation caused you trouble, you said the same words: اَللّٰهُمَّ اغْفِرْ لِقَوْمِيْ فَاِنَّهُمْ لَا يَعْلَمُوْنَ "*O Allah! Forgive*

1 *[Kanz-ul-Iman (translation of Quran)] (Part 29, Surah Nooh, Verse 26)*

my nation because they do not know about me."

O Prophet of Allah صَلَّى اللهُ عَلَيْهِ وَاٰلِهٖ وَسَلَّم! May my mother and father be sacrificed for you! After the declaration of the Prophethood in a short period of time, people believed in you and started following you, whereas it did not happen to Sayyiduna Nuh عَلَيْهِ السَّلَام, although he lived a long life and preached for a long time. A large number of people have believed in you in your lifetime, whereas the number of people who believed in Sayyiduna Nuh عَلَيْهِ السَّلَام is very less.

Chapter 12

Family, Relatives and Friends of the Holy Prophet ﷺ

Family of the Prophet ﷺ[1]

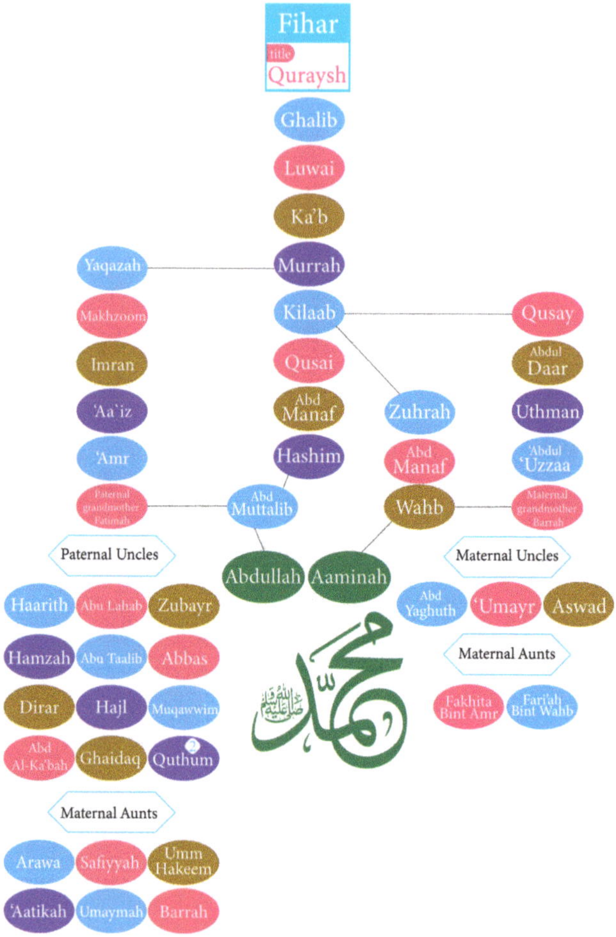

1 This map of the Family of the Prophet has been made with the help of the different pages of as-Sirah an-Nabawiyyah of Ibn Hisham vol. 1, al-Mawahib al-Ladunniyyah vol. 1, Subul al-Huda war-Rashad vol. 1, and Sharh al-Zurqani 'Ala al-Mawahib vol. 4.

2 There is a difference of opinion about the number of the uncles of the Beloved Prophet ﷺ. We have mentioned all the names. Biographers have a consensus on the first nine names, whereas the last three names have been mentioned by the author of Mawahib al-Ladunniyyah with reference to Dhakhaair al-Uqba fee Manaqib Dhawi al-Qura.

Milk relatives *of the* Beloved Prophet صلى الله عليه وسلم[1]

Milk father

Harith Bin Abdul 'Uzza

Milk mothers

Sayyidah Aaminah

The Beloved Prophet's صلى الله عليه وآله وسلم mother, Sayyidah Aaminah رضي الله عنها, suckled him for 7 days.

Haleemah Sa'diyya

Our Beloved Prophet صلى الله عليه وآله وسلم spent most of his period of suckling and also his childhood at her home. When she came to the Beloved Prophet صلى الله عليه وآله وسلم, he صلى الله عليه وآله وسلم spread his own shawl for her.

Umm Farwa

A woman of Banu Sa'd

Sayyiduna Hamzah رضي الله عنه also suckled from her. Therefore, he is also the milk brother of the Beloved Prophet صلى الله عليه وآله وسلم, as well as his uncle.

Sayyidah Thuwaybah

She was the maidservant of Abu Lahab. The Beloved Prophet صلى الله عليه وآله وسلم and Sayyidah Khadija رضي الله عنها would greatly respect her. He صلى الله عليه وآله وسلم would also send clothes, etc., to her from Madinah al-Munawwarah.

Two women from Banu Sulaym

When he صلى الله عليه وآله وسلم was being taken to Banu Sa'd, these women nursed him that time.

Milk brothers

Sayyiduna Hamza

Who is his paternal uncle and also his milk brother.

Abu Sufyan bin Harith

The paternal cousin of the Beloved Prophet صلى الله عليه وآله وسلم; in the beginning, he was against Islam, but then embraced Islam at a later stage

Abu Salamah bin Abdul Asad

He is amongst those who embraced Islam in the early days. Sayyidah Thuwaybah suckled Sayyiduna Hamza and Abu Salamah along with the Beloved Prophet صلى الله عليه وآله وسلم.

Masrooh bin Thuwaybah

The son of Thuwaybah, who was the milk mother of the Beloved Prophet صلى الله عليه وآله وسلم.

Hafs bin Harith

Abdullah bin Harith, the son of Sayyidah Haleemah; some have written his name as Damrah.

Milk brothers

Unaysah bint Harith

The daughter of Sayyidah Haleemah.

Shaymaa bint Harith

The daughter of Sayyidah Haleemah.The latter would greatly take care of the Beloved Prophet صلى الله عليه وآله وسلم in his childhood. When she came to the Beloved Prophet صلى الله عليه وآله وسلم, he صلى الله عليه وآله وسلم spread his shawl for her, and giving her gifts, bid her farewell.

1 This information has been taken from different pages of as-Sirah an-Nabawiyyah of Ibn Hisham vol. 1, al-Mawahib al-Ladunniyyah vol. 1, and Subul al-Huda war-Rashad vol. 1.

Mothers of Believers[1]

Blessed names	*Nikah* with the Beloved Prophet	Age at the time of *Nikah*	Time spent with the Beloved Prophet	Age at the time of blessed passing
Sayyidah Khadija bint Khuwaylid	28 years before the migration	40 years	25 years	65 years
Sayyidah Saudah bint-Zama'ah	3 years before the migration	--------	14 years	--------
Sayyidah 'Aisha bint Abu Bakr Siddeeq	2 years before the migration, and left for his house in the 1st Hijri.	At the time of *Nikah*, 6 years, and at the time of leaving to his house, 9 years.	10 years	65 years
Sayyidah Hafsa bint Umar Farooq	3 Hijri	21 years	8 years	63 years
Sayyidah Zainab bint Khuzaymah	3 Hijri	29 years	8 months	30 years
Sayyidah Umm Salamah bint Abu Umayya	4 Hijri	28 years	7 years	85 years
Sayyidah Zainab bint Jahsh	5 Hijri	37 years	6 years	53 years
Sayyidah Umm Habiba bint Abu Sufyan	6 Hijri	32 years	5 years	69 years
Sayyidah Juwayriya bint Harith	5 Hijri	19 years	6 years	70 years
Sayyidah Maymuna bint Harith[2]	7 Hijri	36 years	4 years	80 years
Sayyidah Safiyya bint Huyay	7 Hijri	16 years	4 years	59 years

1 This information has been taken from 'Sharh al-Zurqaani 'Ala al-Mawahib vol. 4, Usd al-Ghabah vol. 7, Subul Al-Huda Wal-Rashad vol. 4 and Al-Mukhtasar al-Kabir fi Seerat-ar-Rasool'.

2 The real name of Sayyidah Juwayriyah and Sayyidah Maymuna was Barrah. The Beloved Prophet صَلَّى اللّٰهُ عَلَيْهِ وَاٰلِهٖ وَسَلَّم changed this name. Their respective fathers are two different people who both shared the same name, Harith.

Blessed Offspring

Blessed names	Birth	Husband	Offspring	Date of demise	Age at the time of passing
Sayyiduna Qasim	-----------	-----------	-----------	-----------	-----------
Sayyidah Zainab	At 30[1]	Abu Al-Aas bin Rabi	Son: Ali Daughter: Umama	8th Hijri	31 years
Sayyidah Ruqayya	At 33	First Utbah bin Abu Lahab, second Uthman al-Ghani	Son: Abdullah	Ramadan 2nd Hijri	22 years
Sayyidah Umm Kulthoom	At 34	First Utaybah bin Abu Lahab, second Uthman al-Ghani	None	Ramadan 9th Hijri	28 years
Sayyidah Fatima	At 35	Ali Al-Murtaza	Sons: Hasan, Husain, Muhsin Daughters: Zainab, Umm Kulthoom, Ruqayya	3rd Ramadan 11th Hijri	29 years
Sayyiduna Abdullah	After the Declaration of Prophethood	-----------	-----------	4th year of the Declaration of Prophethood	In childhood
Sayyiduna Ibrahim	Zul-Hijjah 8 Hijri[2]	-----------	-----------	10th Rabi-ul-Awwal, 10 Hijri	17 or 18 months

1 Meaning the age of the Beloved Prophet صَلَّى اللّٰهُ عَلَيْهِ وَاٰلِهٖ وَسَلَّم at the time of the birth of that child.

2 This son was born to Sayyidah Mariya. Apart from him, all the sons and daughters of the Beloved Prophet صَلَّى اللّٰهُ عَلَيْهِ وَاٰلِهٖ وَسَلَّم were born to Sayyidah Khadija.

Ghazawaat (battles) and Saraya (expeditions) of the Beloved Prophet صَلَّى اللّٰهُ عَلَيْهِ وَاٰلِهٖ وَسَلَّم

It has been said that the number of battles which took place in the blessed era of the Beloved Rasool صَلَّى اللّٰهُ عَلَيْهِ وَاٰلِهٖ وَسَلَّم is 100. Many of them are such battles in which the need to even lift a sword did not arise. According to some research, in all these *Ghazawaat* and *Saraya*, 181 blessed companions were martyred, whereas 202 non-Muslims were killed. In this way, the total number of people who died in them is 383. From this, it has become obvious that the *Ghazawaat* and *Saraya* which took place in the age of the Beloved Prophet صَلَّى اللّٰهُ عَلَيْهِ وَاٰلِهٖ وَسَلَّم were for the pursuit of peace and safety. The statistics of the *Ghazawaat* and *Saraya* are as follows:

Name of the Battle	Muslims who were martyred	Disbelievers who were killed
The Ghazwah of Badr	14	70
The Ghazwah of Saweeq	02	-
The Sariyya of pursuing Ka'ab bin Ashraf	-	01
The Ghazwah of Uhud	70	22
The Ghazwah of Hamra al-Asad		01
The Sariyya of Raji'	07	-
The Sariyya of Bir Ma'oona	27	-
The Ghazwah of Trench	06	03
The Sariyya Abdullah bin Ateeq	-	01
The Ghazwah of Banu Quraydha	-	-
The Ghazwah of Dhi Qarad	02	01
The Ghazwah of Banu Muṣtaliq	01	-
The Ghazwah of Khayber	20	02
The Ghazwah of Wadi Qura	01	-

The Ghazwah of Mu'tah	11	-
The Conquest of Makkah	03	17
The Ghazwah of Hunain	04	84
The Ghazwah of Taif	13	01
Total	181	202

The Beloved Prophet صَلَّى اللّٰهُ عَلَيْهِ وَاٰلِهٖ وَسَلَّم reached Banu Quraydha with an army in order to punish the Jews for breaking their pact. The Jews became exasperated by the siege and finally surrendered and said that Sayyiduna Sa'ad bin Mu'adh should make a decision about them. In the light of the decision made by Sayyiduna Sa'ad, those who fought for them were killed. In this way, these deaths did not occur in the battlefield.

Some things which were *in the* general use *of the* Beloved Prophet صلى الله عليه وسلم [1]

Scissors

(named Jami')

A kohl bottle

(in order to use it to apply Ithmid kohl at the time of sleeping), a kohl stick (made of wood for applying kohl)

Kohl stick

A wooden stick for applying kohl

A stick

(named Mamshuq)

A small box

(King Muqawqis sent it as a gift. It used to be with the Beloved Prophet صلى الله عليه واله وسلم during journeys; it contained five things: a comb, a kohl bottle, scissors, a Miswak, and a mirror).

A tub

(a brass utensil used for washing clothes).

A large brass utensil

(named Sa'ah)

A staff

(due to which he is referred to as 'Sahib al-Hirawah')

A traditional woven bed

(which was in the home of Sayyidatuna Aaishah رضي الله عنها. It was presented by As'ad bin Zurarah and its legs were made of teak.)

A leather pillow

(stuffed with date tree bark)

Leather bedding

(stuffed with date tree bark)

Mikhdab

(a large tray made of stone with which he صلى الله عليه واله وسلم would perform Wudu).

A mirror

(named Mudilla)

A comb

(made of ivory).

Blessed sandals

(were made of hairless leather with two shoelaces on each for tying).

A chair

(whose legs were made of iron or dark wood).

A dining mat

(at which he صلى الله عليه واله وسلم would sit and eat food).

A mat on which he صلى الله عليه واله وسلم would offer Salah in the night and sit during the day.

Imamas

(black, grey, yellow saffron, white, red striped, green)

1 Sharh al-Zurqani 'Ala al-Mawahib, vol. 5, pg. 93-97

RIDING ANIMALS OF BELOVED PROPHET ﷺ

She-camels	Mule	Donkey
Qaswa, Adba, Jad'a	Duldul	Yafoor[1]

Camels

Salab	Jamal Ahmar	Askar	Sahri	And many camels whose names are not well-known.

White rooster

Goats

Ten goats which would give milk;
Sayyidah Umm Ayman would take them to graze.

Barakah	Zamzam	Qamar	Warshah	Ujrah	Atraaf
Suqy'a	Atlal	Yaman	Ghawtha or Ghaytha		

Twenty milk-giving camels would graze out of Madinah and 2 large leather pouches of milk would be brought daily at night.[2]

1 Subul al-Huda war-Rashad, Chapter on his Animals, vol. 11, pg. 419-420

2 Sharh al-Zurqani 'Ala al-Mawahib vol. 5, pg. 109-112

Chapter 13

The Prophetic Biography at a Glance

Islamic calendar	Gregorian calendar	Important Events
Year of blessed birth	20-04-571	Born on 12th *Rabi' al-Awwal* in Makkah. Passing of father 6 months before the blessed birth.
2nd year	572	Stayed with Sayyidah Haleemah رَضِىَ اللّٰهُ عَنۡهَا in the tribe Banu Sa'd.
3rd year	573	Returned to Makkah, but further stayed in the tribe Banu Sa'd due to an epidemic.
4th Year	574	Splitting of the blessed chest in the tribe Banu Sa'd. Returned to mother.
6th Year	576-577	His mother, Sayyidah Aaminah رَضِىَ اللّٰهُ عَنۡهَا, passed away and was buried in Abwa when he was returning from Madinah with his mother and Umm Ayman.
8th Year	578-579	Passing of Abdul Muttalib (paternal grandfather). Beginning of custodianship of his uncle, Abu Talib.
9th Year	579-580	Severe famine in Arab came to an end by virtue of his blessing.
10th Year	581	Journey to Yemen with his uncle, Zubair, at the age of 10.
12th Year	583	First business trip to Syria with Abu Talib and meeting with Bahira, the Monk.
14th Year	584-585	Attended the Fijar war.
20th Year	589-590	Attended Hilful Fudul.

25th Year	595	Second business trip to the Levant at Sayyidatuna Khadija's request with her goods, and then marrying her after 3 months.
30th Year	600	Birth of Sayyidatuna Zainab رَضِیَ اللهُ عَنْهَا, the eldest daughter of the Prophet.
33rd Year	603	Birth of Sayyidatuna Ruqayya رَضِیَ اللهُ عَنْهَا, the second daughter of the Prophet.
35th Year	605	Participated in the construction of the Kab'ah. Settled the conflict regarding Hajr al-Aswad. Birth of Sayyidatuna Fatima رَضِیَ اللهُ عَنْهَا.
1st Nabawi	Feb. 610	First Divine revelation and declaration of Prophethood at the age of forty.
1st to 3rd Nabawi	610-613	Invitation to Islam secretly for three years. Nikah of the daughter, Sayyidatuna Ruqayya رَضِیَ اللهُ عَنْهَا, with Sayyiduna Uthman al-Ghani رَضِیَ اللهُ عَنْهُ.
4th Nabawi	613-614	Started preaching Islam openly, and started preventing from polytheism and idol worshipping.
5th Nabawi	615	Ordered Muslims to migrate to Abyssinia.
6th Nabawi	616	Sayyiduna Umar al-Farooq رَضِیَ اللهُ عَنْهُ and Sayyiduna Ameer Hamza رَضِیَ اللهُ عَنْهُ embraced Islam.
7th Nabawi	617	Start of the siege of the family of Banu Hashim in the Shi'b of Abi Talib.
10th Nabawi	619-620	End of the boycott in the Shi'b of Abi Talib.

10th Nabawi	619-620	This year is referred to as "'Aam al-Huzn" (the year of grief). His uncle, Abu Talib, and his honourable wife, Sayyidah Khadija رَضِیَ اللّٰہُ عَنْہَا, passed away.
12th Nabawi	July 621	First pledge of 'Aqabah took place when twelve people of Madinah embraced Islam in the narrow valley of Mina. Miracle of Mi'raj was bestowed.
13th Nabawi	June 622	Second pledge of 'Aqabah took place when further seventy-two people took allegiance at his blessed hand in the narrow valley of Mina. Same year in September, he صَلَّی اللّٰہُ عَلَیْہِ وَاٰلِہٖ وَسَلَّم migrated to Madinah.
Rabi' al-Awwal 1st Hijri	622	Arrived in Quba. Construction of Masjid Quba. Offered the first Jumu'ah Salah. Went to Madinah. Constructed Masjid al-Nabawi. Established brotherhood in Madinah. Start of Adhan and Iqamah. His marriage with Sayyidah 'Aisha رَضِیَ اللّٰہُ عَنْہَا. The marriage of Sayyidah Fatima رَضِیَ اللّٰہُ عَنْہَا.

Hijri 2	623-624	Change of the Qiblah. Fasts of Ramadan became obligatory. 'Eid Salahs and Qurbani became Wajib. The Battle of Badr. Birth of Imam Hasan رَضِيَ اللهُ عَنْهُ. Passing of Sayyidah Ruqayya رَضِيَ اللهُ عَنْهَا. The marriage of Sayyidatuna Umm Kulthoom رَضِيَ اللهُ عَنْهَا with Sayyiduna Uthman رَضِيَ اللهُ عَنْهُ.
Shawal 3 Hijri	March 625	The Battle of Uhud. Sayyiduna Hamza رَضِيَ اللهُ عَنْهُ was martyred.
Hijri 4	626 - 625	Incident of Raji' and Bir Ma'una. Command for Salat-ul-Khauf. Birth of Imam Hussain رَضِيَ اللهُ عَنْهُ. His marriages with Sayyidatuna Umm Salama and Sayyidatuna Zainab bint Jahsh رَضِيَ اللهُ عَنْهُمَا. Revelation of Qasr Salah and commandments of veiling.
Hijri 5	626-627	Nikah with Sayyidatuna Juwayriya رَضِيَ اللهُ عَنْهَا. The Battle of the Trench. The Battle of Banu Mustaliq. Incident of Ifk. Commandment of Tayyamum was revealed. The Battle of Banu Quraydha.

Hijri 6	628	The pledge of Ridwan. Treaty of Hudaybiyyah. Sent letters of invitation to Islam to the kings. The honourable Najashi, the king of Abyssinia, embraced Islam.
Hijri 7	628-629	The Battle of Khayber and the Battle of Zat al-Riqa'. Nikah with Sayyidatuna Umm Habibah, Sayyidatuna Safiyya and Sayyidatuna Maymuna رَضِيَ اللّٰهُ عَنْهُنَّ. Miracle of the sun returning after setting. Birth of his son, Sayyiduna Ibrahim رَضِيَ اللّٰهُ عَنْهُ. Performed Qada Umrah.
Hijri 8	630	The Conquest of Makkah. The Battle of Hunain. The Battle of Taif. The Battle of Mu'tah.
Hijri 9	631	The Battle of Tabuk. Different delegations came to the Beloved Prophet صَلَّى اللّٰهُ عَلَيْهِ وَاٰلِهٖ وَسَلَّم.

Hijri 10	632	Passing of his son, Sayyiduna Ibrahim رَضِیَ اللّٰہُ عَنْہُ. Farewell Hajj with a huge congregation of companions. Preparation for the army of Usama. Blessed passing of the Beloved Prophet صَلَّى اللّٰهُ عَلَيْهِ وَاٰلِهٖ وَسَلَّم at the age of 63 years on Monday 12th Rabi' al-Awwal, corresponding to 12th June 632 C.E. (according to another opinion, this took place on 1st Rabi al-Awwal or 2nd Rabi al-Awwal). Blessed burial in the blessed chamber of Sayyidatuna 'Aisha رَضِیَ اللّٰہُ عَنْہَا.

Care has been taken to give exact dates for incidents from the sublime Prophetic biography, however, the possibility of some inaccuracy remains.

Making a home Masjid is a Sunnah

In this book, you will find:

- Designating a place for Salah in the house is a Sunnah
- Who built the first Masjid-e-Bayt in Madinah?
- Masjid-e-Bayt of the Holy Prophet صَلَّى اللهُ عَلَيْهِ وَاٰلِهٖ وَسَلَّم
- 10 accounts about Masjid-e-Bayt

www.ingramcontent.com/pod-product-compliance
Lightning Source LLC
LaVergne TN
LVHW051922051126
851857LV00021B/2103
* 9 7 8 9 6 9 7 2 2 3 6 5 7 *